TOWER HAMLETS COLLEGE

014869

KT-450-252

Withdrawn

Selected Poems 1967-1987

ROGER McGOUGH

Selected Poems 1967-1987

TOWER HAMLETS COLLEGE LIBRARY
POPLAR CENTRE

JONATHAN CAPE

LONDON

First published 1989
Reprinted 1989, 1991
This collection © Roger McGough 1989
Jonathan Cape, 20 Vauxhall Bridge Road, London SW1V 2SA

A CIP catalogue record for this book is available from the
British Library

ISBN 0-224-02718-2

'My Busseductress' and 'Soil' first appeared in *Twentieth Century*, 3rd issue, 1968; 'George and the dragonfly' and 'tightrope' were first published in a limited edition by Turret Books, 1972; 'Three Rusty Nails' was first published under the title of 'Mother, there's a strange man' in *The Liverpool Scene* by Donald Carroll Ltd, 1967; 'Six Shooters' first appeared in *Ambit*. The series of thirteen poems entitled 'Unlucky For Some' was first published by Turret Books; quotation of the newspaper report in 'Rabbit in Mixer Survives' is reproduced by permission of the *Daily Telegraph*.

The following collections were first published by Jonathan Cape © Roger McGough: *Watchwords*, 1969; *After the Merrymaking*, 1971; *Gig*, 1973; *In the Glassroom*, 1976; *Holiday on Death Row*, 1979; *Waving at Trains*, 1982.

The Mersey Sound, 1967 and *Melting into the Foreground*, 1986 were first published by Penguin Books Ltd, © Roger McGough; *Summer with Monika*, 1967 was first published by Michael Joseph Ltd, © Roger McGough; *Nailing the Shadow*, 1987 was first published by Viking Kestrel, © Roger McGough.

Order No:

Class: 821 9

Accession No: 014869

Type:

Photoset by Falcon Graphic Art Ltd
Wallington, Surrey
Printed in Great Britain by
Mackays of Chatham PLC, Chatham, Kent

*To the memory of my
mother and father*

Introduction

With the exception of *Watchwords* which Jonathan
Cape stopped reprinting in August 1983 at my request,
all my books are available. Why then make a selection?

The publication of *Melting into the Foreground* by
Penguin in 1987 marked the passing of two decades
since my first book appeared and it seemed opportune
to present in two volumes those poems which I regard
as my best (those in the second volume having been
chosen with younger readers in mind). Although
generally resisting the temptation to tinker, I have
reworked a few poems because they niggled me into
doing so.

My thanks to Tessa Sayle, Tony Lacey, Frances
Coady, Tom Maschler and A. D. Peters for helping to
make this selection possible, and special thanks to all
who have bought the books and attended the readings
over the years.

Roger McGough
London, 1989

Contents

The Mersey Sound (1967)

Let Me Die a Youngman's Death   15
Comeclose and Sleepnow   16
Aren't We All?   17
A Lot of Water has Flown under your Bridge   18
A Square Dance   20
On Picnics   22
Mother the Wardrobe is Full of Infantrymen   23
Icarus Allsorts   24
At Lunchtime   26
Motorway   28
Sad Aunt Madge   29
The Fallen Birdman   30
My Busconductor   31
The Icingbus   32
There's Something Sad   33
Vinegar   34
Dreampoem   35
The Fish   36
You and Your Strange Ways   37
What You Are   38

Summer with Monika (1967)

summer with monika   43
ten milk bottles   46
saturdaymorning   47
i have lately learned to swim   48
you squeeze my hand   49
sometimes at dawn   50
you are so very beautiful   51
away from you   52
your finger sadly   53
lastnight   54

said i trusted you   55
monika who's been eating my porrage   56
monika the teathings   57
it all started yesterday evening   58
in october   60

Watchwords (1969)

Snipers   62
Soil   64
The Stranger   66
snowscene   67
when you said goodbye   68
Man the Barricades, the Enemy has let loose his
    Pyjamas!   69
My Busseductress   70
Discretion   72
The Act of Love   73
My cat and i   74

After the Merrymaking (1971)

a cat, a horse and the sun   75
The sun no longer loves me   76
On having no one to write a love poem about   77
after the merrymaking, love?   78
Ex art student   79
Vandal   80
Amateur traumatics   81
Hash Wednesday   82
P.O.W.   83
40 - Love   84
Trenchwarfare   86
Bulletins   87
The Mongrel   88
The Newly Pressed Suit   89
cake   90
and the field screamed 'TRACTOR'   91
Train Crash   92
Head Injury   93

Gig (1973)

The Identification 94
George and the dragonfly 96
happiness 98
un 99
pietà 100
crusader 101
tigerdreams 102
tightrope 103
the failed reveller 104
ghosts of ducks 106
devices 107
creepycrawlies 108
stink 109
unlikely now 110
italic 112
The Golden Treasury of Flesh 113
out of sequence 114

In The Glassroom (1976)

Three Rusty Nails 116
cosy biscuit 117
A Brown Paper Carrierbag 118
He who owns the Whistle, rules the World 119
Catching up on Sleep 120

Holiday on Death Row (1979)

Nocturne 121
The Lake 122
The death of John Berryman in slow motion 124
Take a poem, Miss Smith. 125
His poems are nets 126
Blazing Fruit 128
Poem for a dead poet 129
Mouth 130
Cabbage 132
War of the Roses 134
Survivor 135

Just another Autumn day   136
Incident at a Presidential Garden Party   137
May Ball   138
Closet Fascist   139
Solarium   140
Passion   141
The Horse's Mouth   142
A Golden Life   144
The Rot   146
10 Ways to Make a Killing   147
Holiday on Death Row   148

Waving at Trains (1982)
Rabbit in Mixer Survives   160
Six Shooters   164
Happy Ending   170
There Was a Knock on the Door. It Was the Meat.   171
The Birderman   172
When I Am Dead   174
A Visit to the Poet and his Wife   175
The Examination   176
Framed   177
Noah's Arc   178
Waving at Trains   180
Kisses and Blows   181
What My Lady Did   182
Romantic   183
You and I   184
Unlucky For Some   185

Melting into the Foreground (1986)
A Cautionary Calendar   198
The Jogger's Song   200
The End of Summer   202
A Fair Day's Fiddle   203
The Filmmaker   204
Happy Birthday   205

Last Lullaby   206
All Over bar the Shouting   207
Q   208
Who Can Remember Emily Frying?   209
The Host   210
Sap   212
Here I Am   213
Today is Not a Day for Adultery   214
Bits of Me   215
Poem with a Limp   216
Melting into the Foreground   218
In Transit   220
A Joy to be Old   221
Bars are Down   223
My Little Eye   224
Bye Bye Black Sheep   225
Tramp Tramp Tramp   226
Hearts and Flowers   228

Nailing the Shadow (1987)

Hundreds and Thousands   222

Index of First Lines   233

Let Me Die a Youngman's Death

Let me die a youngman's death
not a clean and inbetween
the sheets holywater death
not a famous-last-words
peaceful out of breath death

When I'm 73
and in constant good tumour
may I be mown down at dawn
by a bright red sports car
on my way home
from an allnight party

Or when I'm 91
with silver hair
and sitting in a barber's chair
may rival gangsters
with hamfisted tommyguns burst in
and give me a short back and insides

Or when I'm 104
and banned from the Cavern
may my mistress
catching me in bed with her daughter
and fearing for her son
cut me up into little pieces
and throw away every piece but one

Let me die a youngman's death
not a free from sin tiptoe in
candle wax and waning death
not a curtains drawn by angels borne
'what a nice way to go' death

Comeclose and Sleepnow

it is afterwards
and you talk on tiptoe
happy to be part
of the darkness
lips becoming limp
a prelude to tiredness.
Comeclose and Sleepnow
for in the morning
when a policeman
disguised as the sun
creeps into the room
and your mother
disguised as birds
calls from the trees
you will put on a dress of guilt
and shoes with broken high ideals
and refusing coffee
run
alltheway
home.

Aren't We All?

Looks quite pretty lying there
Can't be asleep yet
Wonder what she's thinking about?
Penny for her thoughts
Probably not worth it.
There's the moon trying to look romantic
Moon's too old that's her trouble
Aren't we all?

Lace curtains gently swaying
Like a woman walking
A woman ina negligee
Walking out through the window
Over the sleeping city up into the sky
To give the moon a rest
Moon's too tired that's her trouble
Aren't we all?

Wasn't a bad party really
Except for the people
People always spoil things
Room's in a mess
And this one's left her clothes allover the place
Scattered like seeds
In too much of a hurry that's her trouble
Aren't we all?

Think she's asleep now
It makes you sleep
Better than Horlicks
Not so pretty really when you get close-up
Wonder what her name is?
Now she's taken all the blankets
Too selfish that's her trouble
Aren't we all?

A Lot of Water has Flown under your Bridge

i remember your hands
white and strangely cold
asif exposed too often to the moon

i remember your eyes
brown and strangely old
asif exposed too often and too soon

i remember your body
young and strangely bold
asif exposed too often

i remember
i remember how
when you laughed
hotdogmen allover town
burst into song

i remember
i remember how
when you cried
the clouds cried too and the
streets became awash with tears

i remember
i remember how
when we lay together for the first time
the room smiled,
said: 'excuse me',
and tiptoed away

but time has passed since then
and alotof people
have crossed over the bridge
(a faceless throng)
but time has passed since then
and alotof youngmen
have swum in the water
(naked and strong)

but time has passed since then
and alotof water
   has flown
     under
      your
        bridge.

A Square Dance

In Flanders fields in Northern France
They're all doing a brand new dance
It makes you happy and out of breath
And it's called the Dance of Death

Everybody stands in line
Everybody's feeling fine
We're all going to a hop
1-2-3 and over the top

It's the dance designed to thrill
It's the mustard gas quadrille
A dance for men — girls have no say in it
For your partner is a bayonet

See how the dancers sway and run
To the rhythm of the gun
Swing your partner dos-y-doed
All around the shells explode

Honour your partner form a square
Smell the burning in the air
Over the barbed wire kicking high
Men like shirts hung out to dry

If you fall that's no disgrace
Someone else will take your place
'Old soldiers never die . . .'
                              . . . Only young ones

In Flanders fields where mortars blaze
They're all doing the latest craze
Khaki dancers out of breath
Doing the glorious Dance of Death
Doing the glorious Dance of Death.

On Picnics

at the goingdown of the sun
and in the morning
i try to remember them
but their names are ordinary names
and their causes are thighbones
tugged excitedly from the soil
by frenchchildren
on picnics

Mother the Wardrobe is Full of Infantrymen

mother the wardrobe is full of infantrymen
i did i asked them
but they snarled saying it was a mans life

mother there is a centurian tank in the parlour
i did i asked the officer
but he laughed saying 'Queens regulations'
(piano was out of tune anyway)

mother polish your identity bracelet
there is a mushroom cloud in the backgarden
i did i tried to bring in the cat
but it simply came to pieces in my hand
i did i tried to whitewash the windows
but there weren't any
i did i tried to hide under the stairs
but i couldn't get in for civil defence leaders
i did i tried ringing candid camera
but they crossed their hearts

i went for a policeman but they were looting the town
i went out for a fire engine but they were all upside down
i went for a priest but they were all on their knees
mother don't just lie there say something please
mother don't just lie there say something please

Icarus Allsorts

*'A meteorite is reported to have landed
in New England. No damage is said . . .'*

A littlebit of heaven fell
From out the sky one day
It landed in the ocean
Not so very far away
The General at the radar screen
Rubbed his hands with glee
And grinning pressed the button
That started World War Three

From every corner of the earth
Bombs began to fly
There were even missile jams
No traffic lights in the sky
In the time it takes to blow your nose
The people fell, the mushrooms rose

'House!' cried the fatlady
As the bingohall moved to various parts
Of the town

'Raus!' cried the German butcher
As his shop came tumbling down

Philip was in the countinghouse
Counting out his money
The Queen was in the parlour
Eating bread and honey
When through the window
Flew a bomb
And made them go all funny

In the time it takes to draw a breath
Or eat a toadstool, instant death

The rich
Huddled outside the doors of their fallout shelters
Like drunken carolsingers

The poor
Clutching shattered televisions
And last week's editions of T.V. Times
(But the very last)

Civil defence volunteers
With their tin hats in one hand
And their heads in the other

C.N.D. supporters
Their ban the bomb badges beginning to rust
Have scrawled 'I told you so' in the dust

A littlebit of heaven fell
From out the sky one day
It landed in Vermont
North-Eastern U.S.A.
The general at the radar screen
He should have got the sack
But that wouldn't bring
Three thousand million, seven hundred,
and sixty-eight people back,
Would it?

At Lunchtime

When the bus stopped suddenly
to avoid damaging
a mother and child in the road,
the younglady in the green hat sitting opposite,
was thrown across me,
and not being one to miss an opportunity
i started to make love.

At first, she resisted,
saying that it was too early in the morning,
and too soon after breakfast,
and anyway, she found me repulsive.
But when i explained
that this being a nuclearage
the world was going to end at lunchtime,
she took off her green hat,
put her busticket into her pocket
and joined in the exercise.

The buspeople,
and there were many of them,
were shockedandsurprised,
and amusedandannoyed.
But when word got around
that the world was going to end at lunchtime,
they put their pride in their pockets
with their bustickets
and made love one with the other.
And even the busconductor,
feeling left out,
climbed into the cab,
and struck up some sort of relationship with the driver.

That night,
on the bus coming home,
we were all a little embarrassed.
Especially me and the younglady in the green hat.
And we all started to say
in different ways
how hasty and foolish we had been.
But then, always having been a bitofalad,
i stood up and said it was a pity
that the world didnt nearly end every lunchtime,
and that we could always pretend.
And then it happened . . .

Quick asa crash
we all changed partners,
and soon the bus was aquiver
with white, mothball bodies doing naughty things.

And the next day
and everyday
In everybus
In everystreet
In everytown
In everycountry

People pretended
that the world was coming to an end at lunchtime.
It still hasnt.
Although in a way it has.

Motorway

The politicians,
(who are buying huge cars with hobnailed wheels
the size of merry-go-rounds)
have a new plan.
They are going to
put cobbles
in our eyesockets
and pebbles
in our navels
and fill us up
with asphalt
and lay us
side by side
so that we can take a more active part
in the road
to destruction.

Sad Aunt Madge

As the cold winter evenings drew near
Aunt Madge used to put extra blankets
over the furniture, to keep it warm and cosy
Mussolini was her lover, and life
was an outoffocus rosy-tinted spectacle

but neurological experts
with kind blueeyes
and gentle voices
small white hands
and large Rolls Royces
said that electric shock treatment
should do the trick
it did . . .

today after 15 years of therapeutic tears
and an awful lot of ratepayers' shillings
down the hospital meter
sad Aunt Madge
no longer tucks up the furniture
before kissing it goodnight
and admits
that her affair with Mussolini
clearly was not right
particularly in the light
of her recently announced engagement
to the late pope.

The Fallen Birdman

The oldman in the cripplechair
Died in transit through the air
And slopped into the road.

The driver of the lethallorry
Trembled out and cried: 'I'm sorry,
But it was his own fault'.

Humans snuggled round the mess
In masochistic tenderness
As raindrops danced in his womb.

* * *

But something else obsessed my brain,
The canvas, twistedsteel and cane,
His chair, spreadeagled in the rain,
Like a fallen birdman.

My Busconductor

My busconductor tells me
he only has one kidney
and that may soon go on strike
through overwork.
Each busticket
takes on now a different shape
and texture.
He holds a ninepenny single
as if it were a rose
and puts the shilling in his bag
as a child into a gasmeter.
His thin lips
have no quips
for fat factorygirls
and he ignores
the drunk who snores
and the oldman who talks to himself
and gets off at the wrong stop.
He goes gently to the bedroom
of the bus
to collect
and watch familiar shops and pubs passby
(perhaps for the last time?)
The sameold streets look different now
more distinct
as through new glasses.
And the sky
was it ever so blue?
And all the time
deepdown in the deserted busshelter of his mind
he thinks about his journey nearly done.
One day he'll clock on and never clock off
or clock off and never clock on.

The Icingbus

the littleman
with the hunchbackedback
creptto his feet
to offer his seat
to the blindlady

people gettingoff
steered carefully around
the black mound
of his back
as they would a pregnantbelly

the littleman
completely unaware
of the embarrassment behind
watched as the blindlady
fingered out her fare
     *   *   *
muchlove later he suggested that instead
ofa wedding-cake they shouldhave a miniaturebus
made outof icing but she laughed
andsaid that buses werefor travelling in
and notfor eating and besides
you cant taste shapes.

There's Something Sad

There's something sad
about the glass
with lipstick on its mouth
that's pointed at and given back
to the waitress in disgust

    Like the girl with the hair-lip
       whom
           no one
              wants
                to
                   kiss.

Vinegar

sometimes
i feel like a priest
in a fish & chip queue
quietly thinking
as the vinegar runs through
how nice it would be
to buy supper for two

Dreampoem

in a corner of my bedroom
 grew a tree
 a happytree
 my own tree
its leaves were soft
 like flesh
and its birds sang poems for me
then
 without warning
two men
 with understanding smiles
and axes
 made out of forged excuses
came and chopped it down
either   yesterday
 or the day before
i think it was the day before

The Fish

you always were a strange girl now weren't you?
like the midsummernights party we went to
where towards witching
being tired and hot of dancing
we slipped thro' the frenchwindows
and arminarmed across the lawn

pausing at the artificial pond
lying liquidblack and limpid
in the stricttempo air we kissed
when suddenly you began to tremble
and removing one lavender satin glove knelt
and slipped your hand into the slimy mirror

your face was sad as you brought forth
a switching twitching silver fish
which you lay at my feet
and as the quick tick of the grass
gave way to the slow flop of death
stillkneeling you said softly: 'don't die little fish'

then you tookoff your other glove
and we lay sadly and we made love
as the dancers danced slowly
the fish stared coldly
and the moon admired its reflection
in the lilypetalled pond

You and Your Strange Ways

increasingly oftennow
you reach into your handbag
(the one I bought some xmasses ago)
and bringing forth
a pair of dead cats
skinned and glistening
like the undersides of tongues
or old elastoplasts
sticky with earwigs
you hurl them at my eyes
and laugh cruellongly
why?
even though we have grown older together
and my kisses are little more than functional
i still love you
you and your strange ways

What You Are

you are the cat's paw
among the silence of midnight goldfish

you are the waves
which cover my feet like cold eiderdowns

you are the teddybear (as good as new)
found beside a road accident

you are the lost day
in the life of a child murderer

you are the underwatertree
around which fish swirl like leaves

you are the green
whose depths I cannot fathom

you are the clean sword
that slaughtered the first innocent

you are the blind mirror
before the curtains are drawn back

you are the drop of dew on a petal
before the clouds weep blood

you are the sweetfresh grass that goes sour
and rots beneath children's feet

you are the rubber glove
dreading the surgeon's brutal hand

you are the wind caught on barbedwire
and crying out against war

you are the moth
entangled in a crown of thorns

you are the apple for teacher
left in a damp cloakroom

you are the smallpox injection
glowing on the torchsinger's arm like a swastika

you are the litmus leaves
quivering on the suntan trees

you are the ivy
which muffles my walls

you are the first footprints in the sand
on bankholiday morning

you are the suitcase full of limbs
waiting in a leftluggage office
to be collected like an orphan

you are a derelict canal
where the tincans whistle no tunes

you are the bleakness of winter before the cuckoo
catching its feathers on a thornbush
heralded spring

you are the stillness of Van Gogh
before he painted the yellow vortex of his last sun

you are the still grandeur of the Lusitania
before she tripped over the torpedo
and laid a world war of american dead
at the foot of the blarneystone

you are the distance
between Hiroshima and Calvary
measured in mother's kisses

you are the distance
between the accident and the telephone box
measured in heartbeats

you are the distance
between power and politicians
measured in half-masts

you are the distance
between advertising and neuroses
measured in phallic symbols

you are the distance
between you and me
measured in tears

you are the moment
before the noose clenched its fist
and the innocent man cried: treason

you are the moment
before the warbooks in the public library
turned into frogs and croaked khaki obscenities

you are the moment
before the buildings turned into flesh
and windows closed their eyes

you are the moment
before the railwaystations burst into tears
and the bookstalls picked their noses

you are the moment
before the buspeople turned into teeth
and chewed the inspector
for no other reason than he was doing his duty

you are the moment
before the flowers turned into plastic and melted
in the heat of the burning cities

you are the moment
before the blindman puts on his dark glasses

you are the moment
before the subconscious begged to be left in peace

you are the moment
before the world was made flesh

you are the moment
before the clouds became locomotives
and hurtled headlong into the sun

you are the moment
before the spotlight moving across the darkened stage
like a crab finds the singer

you are the moment
before the seed nestles in the womb

you are the moment
before the clocks had nervous breakdowns
and refused to keep pace with man's madness

you are the moment
before the cattle were herded together like men

you are the moment
before God forgot His lines

you are the moment of pride
before the fiftieth bead

you are the moment
before the poem passed peacefully away at dawn
like a monarch

summary with monika

they say the sun shone now and again
but it was generally cloudy
with far too much rain

they say babies were born
married couples made love
(often gently)
and people died
(sometimes violently)

they say it was an average
                ordinary
                moderate
                run of the mill
                commonorgarden
                summer
. . . but it wasn't

for i locked a yellowdoor
and i threw away the key
and i spent summer with monika
and monika spent summer with me

unlike everybody else
we made friends with the weather . . .
mostdays the sun called
                and sprawled
allover the place
or the wind blew in
as breezily as ever
and ran its fingers through our hair

but usually
it was the moon that kept us company

somedays we thought about the seaside
and built sandcastles on the blankets
and paddled in the pillows
or swam in the sink
and played with the shoals of dishes

otherdays we went for long walks
around the table
and picnicked on the banks
of the settee
or just sunbathed lazily
in front of the fire
until the shilling set on the horizon

we danced a lot that summer . . .
bosanovaed by the bookcase
or maddisoned instead
hulligullied by the oven
or twisted round the bed

at first we kept birds
in a transistor box
to sing for us
but sadly they died
we being too embraced in eachother
to feed them

but it didn't really matter
because we made lovesongs with our bodies
i became the words
and she put me to music

they say it was just
              like
              anyother
              summer

              . . . but it wasn't

for we had love and eachother
and the moon for company
when i spent summer with monika
and
    monika
      spent summer
        withme

2

ten milk bottles standing in the hall
ten milk bottles up against the wall
next door neighbour thinks we're dead
hasnt heard a sound he said
doesn't know weve been in bed
the ten whole days since we were wed

noone knows and noone sees
we lovers doing as we please
but people stop and point at these
ten milk bottles a-turning into cheese

ten milk bottles standing day and night
ten different thicknesses and
different shades of white
persistent carolsingers without a note to utter
silent carolsingers a-turning into butter

now she's run out of passion
and theres not much left in me
so maybe we'll get up
and make a cup of tea
then people can stop wondering
what they're waiting for
those ten milk bottles a-queuing at our door
those ten milk bottles a-queuing at our door

3

saturdaymorning
time for stretching
and yawning
the languid
heavy lidded
lovemaking
the smile
the kiss
the 'who do you love?'
and then the weekly
confidence trick:
the yoursaying it's my
turn to make the tea
and the my getting out
of bed and making it

6

i have lately learned to swim
and now feel more at home
in the ebb and flow of your slim
rhythmic tide
than in the fullydressed
          couldntcareless
restless world outside

II

you squeeze my hand and
   cry alittle
you cannot comprehend the
   raggletaggle of living
and think it unfair that
   Death
should be the only one
who knows what he's doing

13

sometimes at dawn you awake
and naked creep across our orangeroom
and drawing aside
our prettyyellow curtains
gaze at the neatroofed horizon
of our littletown
waiting for the sun
screaming with dull pain
to rise like a spark
from a crematorium chimney
then you pitterpad back to bed
your head aflame with fear
you lie in my arms
and you lie:
'i'm happy here
so happy here'

16

you are so very beautiful
i cannot help admiring
your eyes so often sadnessful
and lips so kissinspiring

i think about my being-in-love
and touch the flesh you wear so well
i think about my being-in-love
and wish you were as well
              as well
and wish you were as well

18

away from you
i feel a great emptiness
a gnawing loneliness

with you
i get that reassuring feeling
of wanting to escape

26

your finger
sadly
has a familiar ring
about it

34

lastnight
was your night out
and just before you went
you put your SCOWLS
in a tumbler
halffilled with steradent

(so that they'd keep nice and fresh for me)

35

said i trusted you
spoke too soon
heard of your affair
with the maninthemoon
say its allover
then if you're right
why does he call
at the house everynight?

39

monika who's been eating my porrage
while i've been away
my quaker oats are nearly gone
what have you got to say?

someone's been at my whisky
taken the jaguar keys
and monika, another thing
whose trousers are these?

i love and trust you darling
can't really believe you'd flirt
but there's a strange man under the table
wearing only a shirt

there's someone in the bathroom
someone behind the door
the house is full of naked men
monika! don't you love ME anymore?

40

monika the teathings are taking over!
the cups are as big as bubblecars
they throttle round the room
tinopeners skate on the greasy plates
by the light of the silvery moon
the biscuits are having a party
they're necking in our breadbin
thats jazz you hear from the saltcellars
but they don't let nonmembers in
the eggspoons had our eggs for breakfast
the saucebottle's asleep in our bed
i overheard the knives and forks
'it won't be long' they said
'it won't be long' they said

4I

it all started yesterday evening
as i was helping the potatoes
off with their jackets
i heard you making a date
with the kettle
i distinctly
heard you making a date
with the kettle
my kettle

then at midnight
in the halflight
while i was polishing the bluespeckles
in a famous soappowder
i saw you fondling
the fryingpan
i distinctly
saw you fondling the frying pan
my frying pan

finally at middawn
in the halfnight
while waiting in the coolshadows
beneath the sink
i saw you makinglove
with the gascooker
i distinctly
saw you makinglove
with the gascooker
my gascooker

my mistake was to leap upon you crying
'MONIKA THINK OF THE SAUCERS!'
for now i'm alone
you having left me for someone
with a bigger kitchen

42

in october
when winter the lodger the sod
came a-knocking at our door
i set in a store
of biscuits and whisky
you filled the hotwaterbottle with tears
and we went to bed until spring

in april
we arose
warm and smelling of morning
we kissed the sleep from eachothers eyes
and went out into the world

and now summer's here again
regular as the rentman
but our lives are now more ordered more arranged
the kissing wildly carefree times have changed

we nolonger stroll along the beaches of the bed
or snuggle in the longgrass of the carpets
the room nolonger a world for makebelieving in
but a ceiling and four walls that are for living in

we nolonger eat our dinner holding hands
or neck in the backstalls of the television
the room nolonger a place for hideandseeking in
but a container that we use for eatandsleeping in

our love has become
              as comfortable
as the jeans you lounge about in
as my old green coat

              as necessary
as the change you get from the milkman
for a five pound note

our love has become
              as nice
as a cup of tea in bed
              as simple
as something the baby said

monika

    the sky is blue
    the leaves are green
    the birds are singing
    the bells are ringing
    for me and my gal
    the suns as big as an icecream factory
    and the corn is as high as an elephants'
i could go on for hours about the beautiful
weather we're having but monika
    they dont
    make summers
    like they
    used to . . .

Snipers

When I was kneehigh to a tabletop,
Uncle Tom came home from Burma.
He was the youngest of seven brothers
so the street borrowed extra bunting
and whitewashed him a welcome.

All the relations made the pilgrimage,
including us, laughed, sang, made a fuss.
He was as brown as a chairleg,
drank tea out of a white mug the size of my head,
and said next to nowt.

But every few minutes he would scan
the ceiling nervously, hands begin to shake.
'For snipers,' everyone later agreed,
'A difficult habit to break.'

Sometimes when the two of us were alone,
he'd have a snooze after dinner
and I'd keep an eye open for Japs.
Of course, he didn't know this
and the tanner he'd give me before I went
was for keeping quiet,
but I liked to think it was money well spent.

Being Uncle Tom's secret bodyguard
had it's advantages, the pay was good
and the hours were short, but even so,
the novelty soon wore off, and instead,
I started school and became an infant.

Later, I learned that he was in a mental home.
'Needn't tell anybody . . . Nothing serious
. . . Delayed shock . . . Usual sort of thing
. . . Completely cured now the doctors say.'
The snipers came down from the ceiling
but they didn't go away.

Over the next five years they picked off
three of his brothers; one of whom was my father.
No glory, no citations,
Bang! straight through the heart.

Uncle Tom's married now, with a family.
He doesn't say much, but each night after tea,
he still dozes fitfully in his favourite armchair.
He keeps out of the sun, and listens now and then
for the tramp tramp tramp of the Colonel Bogeymen.
He knows damn well he's still at war,
just that the snipers aren't Japs anymore.

Soil

we've ignored eachother for a long time
and I'm strictly an indoor man
anytime to call would be the wrong time
I'll avoid you as long as I can

When I was a boy we were good friends
I made pies out of you when you were wet
And in childhood's remembered summer weather
We roughandtumbled together
We were very close

just me and you and the sun
the world a place for having fun
always so much to be done

But gradually I grew away from you
Of course you were still there
During my earliest sexcapades
When I roughandfumbled
Not very well after bedtime
But suddenly it was winter
And you seemed so cold and dirty
That I stayed indoors and acquired
A taste for girls and clean clothes

we found less and less to say
you were jealous so one day
I simply upped and moved away

I still called to see you on occasions
But we had little now in common
And my visits grew less frequent
Until finally
One coldbright April morning
A handful of you drummed
On my father's waxworked coffin

at last it all made sense
there was no need for pretence
you said nothing in defence

And now recently
While travelling from town to town
Past where you live
I have become increasingly aware
Of you watching me out there.
Patient and unforgiving
Toying with the trees.

we've avoided eachother for a long time
and I'm strictly a city man
anytime to call would be the wrong time
I'll avoid you as long as I can.

The Stranger

'Look quickly!' said the stranger
I turned around in time to see
a wall fall onto the child
playing beside a derelict house
In the silence of the rising dust
I saw the child's arm thrust
out stiff between the bricks
like a tulip
                a white tulip
                                a clenched tulip
I turned angrily to the stranger
'Why did you have to tell me?'
'Well I thought you'd want to see' he said
the tulip screamed
                now limp
                                now red

snowscene

snow crackles underfoot
like powdered bones
trees have dandruff
in their hair
and the wind moans
     the wind moans

ponds are wearingglasses
with lenses three feet deep
birds are silent in the air
as stones
and the wind can't sleep
     the wind can't sleep

i found an oldman by the road
who had not long been dead
i had not heard his lonely groans
nor seen him weep
only birds heard the last words he said
before the wind pulled a sheet o'er his head
     the wind pulled a sheet o'er his head

when you said goodbye

when you said you loved me
the sun
leapt out from behind st georges hall
and ran around town;
        kissing younggirls' faces
        exposing fatmen's braces
        freeing birds & chasing flies
        pulling hats down over eyes
        making bobbies get undressed
        barrowladies look their best
        wayside winos sit and dream
        hotdogmen to sell ice-cream

but when you said goodbye
i heard that the sun
had been runover
somewhere in castle street
by a busload of lovers
whom you have yet to meet

Man the Barricades, the Enemy
has let loose his Pyjamas!

yesterday
secure behind
your barricade
of polite coffeecups
you sat
whittling clichés

but lastnight
slyold me
got you up
some dark alleyway
of my dreams

this morning
you have a   faraway look
in your
smalltalk

My Busseductress

She is as beautiful as bustickets
and smells of old cash
drinks Guinness off duty
eats sausage and mash.
But like everyone else
she has her busdreams too
when the peakhour is over
and there's nothing to do.

A fourposter upstairs
a juke-box inside
there are more ways than one
of enjoying a ride.
Velvet curtains on the windows
thick carpets on the floor
roulette under the stairs
a bar by the door.

Three times a day
she'd perform a strip-tease
and during the applause
say nicely 'fares please'.
Upstairs she'd reserve
for men of her choice
invite them along
in her best clippie voice.

She knows it sounds silly
what would the police say
but thinks we'd be happier
if she had her way.
There are so many youngmen
she'd like to know better
give herself with the change
if only they'd let her.

She is as beautiful as bustickets
and smells of old cash
drinks Guinness off duty
eats sausage and mash.
But she has her busdreams
hot and nervous
my blueserged queen
of the transport service.

Discretion

Discretion is the better part of Valerie
(though all of her is nice)
lips as warm as strawberries
eyes as cold as ice
the very best of everything
only will suffice
not for her potatoes
and puddings made of rice

Not for her potatoes
and puddings made of rice
she takes carbohydrates
like God takes advice
a surfeit of ambition
is her particular vice
Valerie fondles lovers
like a mousetrap fondles mice

And though in the morning
she may whisper: 'it was nice'
you can tell by her demeanour
that she keeps her love on ice
but you've lost your hardearned heart
now you'll have to pay the price
for she'll kiss you on the memory
and vanish in a trice

Valerie is corruptible
but known to be discreet
Valerie rides a silver cloud
where once she walked the street.

The Act of Love

The Act of Love lies somewhere
between the belly and the mind
I lost the love sometime ago
Now I've only the act to grind

Brought her home from a party
don't bother swapping names
identity's not needed
when you're only playing games

High on bedroom darkness
we endure the pantomime
ships that go bang in the night
run aground on the sands of time

Saved in the nick of dawn
its cornflakes and then goodbye
another notch on the headboard
another day wondering why

The Act of Love lies somewhere
between the belly and the mind
I lost the love sometime ago
Now I've only the act to grind.

My cat and i

Girls are simply the prettiest things
My cat and i believe
And we're always saddened
When it's time for them to leave

We watch them titivating
(that often takes a while)
And though they keep us waiting
My cat & i just smile

We like to see them to the door
Say how sad it couldn't last
Then my cat and i go back inside
And talk about the past.

a cat, a horse and the sun

a cat mistrusts the sun
keeps out of its way
only where sun and shadow meet
it moves

a horse loves the sun
it basks all day
snorts
and beats its hooves

the sun likes horses
but hates cats
that is why it makes hay
and heats tin roofs

The sun no longer loves me

The sun no longer loves me.
When i sit waiting for her
in my little room
she arrives
not cheerfully
but out of a sense of duty
like a National Health prostitute.

Sometimes
she leans silky
against the wall
lolling and stretchy
but mostdays she fidgets
and scratches at clouds.
Whenever i ask her to stay the night
she takes umbrage
and is gone.

On having no one to write a love poem about

thismorning
while strolling through my head
rummaging in litterbins
i found by the roadside
an image
that someone had thrown away
A rose

i picked it up
hurried into a backstreet
away from the busy thoroughfare of thoughts
and waited to give it
to the first girl who smiled at me

it's getting dark
and i'm still waiting
The rose attracts a fly

    getting dark
two groupies and a dumb broad
have been the only passersby

      dark
i chance a prayer
There is a smell of tinsel in the air.

after the merrymaking, love?

after the merrymaking,
love.
Back to my place
it's not far
a little shedevil
whoever you are.
It was great fun while I lasted.

after the love,
sleep.
In the onrush of its lava
we are caught
side by side
arms entangled
carcass to carcass.

after the sleep,
emptiness.
The sweat dry
and a little nearer death
we awake to meet the day
we say goodmorning
and I wish you five hundred miles away.

Ex art student

Neat-haired and
low-heeled
you live without passion

hold down
a dull job
in the world of low fashion

ambition
once prickly
is limpid is static

portfolioed
your dreams
lie now in the attic

Vandal

at first
we had a landscape to ourselves
Then the vandals moved in

deflowered the verges
put the carp before the horse
                    and worse
chopped down our initialled trees
bonfired the bench
on which we'd had our first kiss
threw stones
and chased you away

This morning
one of them was caught
He turned out to be me
I am due to appear in court next week
Charged
with emotion

Amateur traumatics

When you starred in *my* play
you were just right
I gave you rave notices
night after night

But you wanted bigger and better parts
Upstarts
sent you script after script
You counted your lines
then you flipped. You just flipped.

Hash Wednesday

last wednesday
   it all clicked

   you only wanted me for my loveandaffection
                        my generosity
                   and my undyingfaithfulness

(to you my prizegiven rosaries meant nothing,
my holy relics, merely relics)

Begone oh Belial's daughter
I wash my hands of you in holy water

next year i will live alone
and breed racehorses
in the attic   —

P.O.W.

it wouldn't be wise to go away together
not even for a weekend.
A few bouts of neocopulation
in a Trust House in the Midlands
would not be the answer.

I commit my sins gentle
Prefer my adultery mental.

Though we feel the need to escape
sometimes
The need for a scape-
goat sometimes
You my muddled tunnel
I your Wooden Horse
We'd only keep running all night
then give ourselves up at first light.

You see I don't love you
And though you're as beautiful as she was
it wouldn't be wise to go away together.
My sense of duty would trouble you
I'm a semi-detached P.O.W.

middle

couple

ten

when

game

and

go

the

will

be

tween

Love

aged

playing

nis

the

ends

thcy

home

net

still

be

them

Trenchwarfare

after the battle of the Incriminating Loveletter
there came an uneasy truce
We still sleep together in the same trench
but you have built
a wall of sandbags in between

somenights
gutsy and fullofight
rifle in hand
I'm over the top
brave asa ram

and you're always waiting,
my naked sentry
'Halt, who goes there? Friend or lover?'
'Lover'
'Advance lover'

in the morning
whistling 'itsalongwaytotipperary'
i trudge across the skyline
to the bathroom

Bulletins

We sit in front of the wireless
waiting for the latest news
on the state of our affair
You knitting socks for our footballers overseas
me wishing i was there
The bulletins are more frequent now
they are broadcast by the hour
The headline in the *Echo* reads
'Love turned Sour'

The Mongrel

When i came to live with you
i brought a brighteyed pup
and as our love matured
so the pup grew up

you fed him and you trained him
asif he were your own
you pampered him looked after him
until he was full grown

then you went away
    now he's uncontrollable
            inconsolable

mistresses they come and go
look pretty much the same
they pat his head and stroke his back
and say they're glad they came

but he's no longer interested
in feminine acclaim
and when they try new tricks
he tires quickly of the game

he skulks around the kitchen
looking old and slightly lame
at night he howls at the window
asif the moon's to blame

and with every sad encounter
i realize to my shame
that my sadeyed mongrel
answers only to your name.

The Newly Pressed Suit

Here is a poem for the two of us to play.
Choose any part from the following:
    The *hero*
    The *heroine*
    The *bed*
    The *bedroom*
    The *newly pressed suit*
(I will play the VILLAIN)

The poem begins this evening at a poetry-reading
Where the *hero* and the *heroine*
Are sitting and thinking of making love.
During the interval, unseen
they slip out and hurry home.
Once inside they waste no time.
The *hero* quickly undresses the *heroine*,
carries her naked into the *bedroom*
and places her gently upon the *bed*
like a *newly pressed suit*.

Just then I step into the poem.
With a sharp left hook
I render unconscious the *hero*
And with a cruel laugh
Leap upon the *heroine*
(The cavortings continue for several stanzas)

Thank you for playing.

When you go out tonight
I hope you have better luck in your poem
Than you had in mine.

cake

i wanted one life
you wanted another
we couldn't have our cake
so we ate eachother.

and the field screamed 'TRACTOR'

harvesttime
the sky
the inside of a giant balloon
sky blue
someone's yellow finger sticking through

late birds screech
wormless

waiting to be threshed
within an inch of its life
the field trembles

the pain
ohthepainoh
the pain

Train Crash

i once met a man
who had been in a crash
during the war

he said the worst thing
was the pause after
and the pause before

the bloody screaming
which though nervesplintttering
might well be heard

most nights on TV
He spoke slowly
pausing   between   each   word

Head Injury

I do not smile because I am happy.
Because I gurgle I am not content.
I feel in colours, mottled, mainly black.
And the only sound I hear is the sea
Pounding against the white cliffs of my skull.

For seven months I lay in a coma.
Agony.
Darkness.
My screams drowned by the wind
Of my imperceptible breathing.

One morning the wind died down. I awoke.

You are with me now as you are everyday
Seeking some glimmer of recognition
Some sign of recovery. You take my hand.
I try to say: 'I love you.'
Instead I squawk,
Eyes bobbing like dead birds in a watertank.
I try to say: 'Have pity on me, pity on yourself
Put a bullet between the birds.'
Instead I gurgle.
You kiss me then walk out of the room.
I see your back.
I feel a colour coming, mottled, mainly black.

The Identification

So you think its Stephen?
Then I'd best make sure
Be on the safe side as it were.
Ah, theres been a mistake. The hair
you see, its black, now Stephens fair . . .
Whats that? The explosion?
Of course, burnt black. Silly of me.
I should have known. Then lets get on.

The face, is that the face I ask?
That mask of charred wood
blistered, scarred could
that have been a child's face?
The sweater, where intact, looks
in fact all too familiar.
But one must be sure.

The scoutbelt. Yes thats his.
I recognise the studs he hammered in
not a week ago. At the age
when boys get clothes-conscious
now you know. Its almost
certainly Stephen. But one must
be sure. Remove all trace of doubt.
Pull out every splinter of hope.

Pockets. Empty the pockets.
Handkerchief? Could be any schoolboy's.
Dirty enough. Cigarettes?
Oh this can't be Stephen.
I dont allow him to smoke you see.
He wouldn't disobey me. Not his father.

But thats his penknife. Thats his alright.
And thats his key on the keyring
Gran gave him just the other night.
So this must be him.

I think I know what happened
. . . . . . about the cigarettes
No doubt he was minding them
for one of the older boys.
Yes thats it.
Thats him.
Thats our Stephen.

George and the dragonfly

Georgie Jennings was spit almighty.
When the golly was good
he could down a dragonfly at 30 feet
and drown a 100 midges with the fallout.
At the drop of a cap
he would outspit lads
years older and twice his size.
Freckled and rather frail
he assumed the quiet dignity
beloved of schoolboy heroes.

But though a legend in his own playtime
Georgie Jennings failed miserably in the classroom
and left school at 15 to work for his father.
And talents such as spitting
are considered unbefitting
for upandcoming porkbutchers.

I haven't seen him since,
but like to imagine some summer soiree
when, after a day moistening mince,
George and his wife entertain tanned friends.
And after dinner, sherrytongued talk
drifts back to schooldays,
the faces halfrecalled, the adventures
overexaggerated. And the next thing
that shy sharpshooter of days gone by
is led, vainly protesting, on to the lawn
where, in the hush of a golden august evening
a reputation, 20 years tall, is put to the test.

So he takes extra care as yesterheroes must,
fires, and a dragonfly, encapsulated, bites the dust.
Then amidst bravos and tinkled applause,
blushing, Georgie leads them back indoors.

happiness

lying in bed ofa weekdaymorning
Autumn
and the trees
none the worse for it.
Youve just got up
to make tea toast and a bottle
leaving pastures warm
for me to stretch into

in his cot
the littlefella
outsings the birds

Plenty of honey in the cupboard.
Nice.

the baby
fourteen months
to the month
moans in the heat
of a summer, come late
with a vengeance.

2 a.m.
and allover the city
bodies sweat
and tingle, the wearers
dancing, wending home,
or fast un asleep.

pietà

in the no mans land
between opening hours
2 winos
compose a pietà

one
asleep on a bench
halfbottle of richruby
warm and safe
in his richruby
winepocket

the other
keeping an eye
on the cathedral.

crusader

in bed
like a dead
crusader

arms a
cross my chest
i lie

eyes closed
listening
to the bodys glib mechanics

* * *

on the street
outside
men of violence

quarrel.
Their drunken voices
dark weals

on the
glistening
back of the night.

i go to sleep on all fours
ready to pounce
on any dream
in which you might appear
Claws withdrawn
i want you live
the image fresh as meat
i want you live
the memories flesh to eat
Every nightmare its the same
prowling through forests
growling your name
until the alarmclock cracks the first twig
and lifting the blankets
i collapse
into the undergrowth.

tightrope

at 7.55 this morning
the circus ran away to join me

there is a lion in the wardrobe
and in the pantry
the clown
goes
   down
     on the bareback rider

the seal in the bath is wearing my hat
and the elephants
have shat on the cat on the mat

my wife (always a dwarf at heart)
juggles naked for the ringmaster
who lashes her approvingly

i stagger out of bed
to shew the tightropewalkers
a thing or two.

the failed reveller

midnight
alone
the failed reveller
wends
his wary way
home

no wind
no people
no cars

sheets of ice
are nailed
to the street
with stars

1 a.m.
i dont miss
my teddy bear
only you
two hands
where its hot
in a bed
made for two

2 a.m.
and the ale
wearing off
so quiet
i can hear
the eggs
in the fridge
shu f f f ling

7 a.m.
alarmclock
sends fireengines
clanging into
my dreams

bedroom is cold
i reach out
and put on
my hangover

ghosts of ducks

All night
ghosts of ducks
longsince plucked
waddled menacingly
across the eiderdown

In the morning
mealyeyed I stood
on the foot of the bed.
The bed yowled
and kicked me across the room

I picked myself up
and took myself out for a walk
(unfortunately we became separated
so I had to come home alone).

devices

Down first for breakfast
in the neat and nic-nac tidy
diningroom I am left to my devices.
I pick up cold steel talons
and tear into the heart of Egg
which bleeds over strips of dead
pig marinated in brine.
Grey shabby Mushrooms squeal
as they are hacked to death
slithering in their own sweat.
Like policemen to a motorway accident,
Toast arrives. The debris is mopped up.
Nothing remains of the slaughter.
John comes in with Judy.
'Mornin'
'Mornin'
'Up early then?'
'Aye'
Life goes on.

spiders are holding their wintersports
in the bathroom. Skating on the
lino, skiing down the slippery
slopes of the bath. Burdened
with my British sense of fairplay
and love of animals, I shower
on tiptoe, water at half-throttle.
I try whistling a happy toon.
The walls, painted in memory
of some longdead canary have
cloth ears: grey cunard towels
folded frayed-side in. Outside
the town too is taking an
evening shower before going out
for the night. Less sensitive
than I to the creepycrawlies
creepingcrawling round its aching feet.

Sometimes I dont smell so good.
Its not that I dont care about
personal hygiene. I do. Its just that
sometimes the body catches up on me.
Like when Im out all day and
refuse to pay for a wash and
brush up at the local municipal
on lack of principle. And hiding
away in some unfamiliar un
kempt saloon I console myself
theres no such thing as *bad* breath.
All breath is good. And sweat
means the body functions as it
should. I drink my bitter.
Put a pork pie to the knife.
Far sweeter than the stink of
death, is the stink of life.

unlikely now

It seems unlikely now
that I shall ever nod in
the winning goal for Everton
and run around Wembley with the cup

unlikely too
that I shall rout
the Aussies at Lords
with my deadly inswingers

that I shall play
the romantic lead in a Hollywood film
based on the Broadway musical
in which I starred

that I shall be a missionary
spreading wisdom
and the Word of God
amongst our pagan brethren

it all seems unlikely now
and so I seek dreams more mundane
ambitions more easily attained
              a day at the seaside
              a poem started
              a change of beard
              an unruly orgasm
              a new tracksuit

and at the end of each day
I count my successes
(adding 10 if I go to bed sober)

by thus keeping one pace ahead of myself
I need never catch up with the truth

It seems unlikely now
that you will enter this room
close the curtains
and turn back the clock.

ONCE I LIVED IN CAPITALS
MY LIFE INTENSELY PHALLIC

but now i'm sadly lowercase
with the occasional *italic*

The Golden Treasury of Flesh

Stoned and lonely in the union bar
looking for a warm student
to fall upon. Someone gentle
and undemanding. History perhaps?
Not Maths or English.

Not English. I'm in
no mood to be laid
alongside our literary heritage
allocated my place in her
golden treasury of flesh.

Geography might do the job.
To snuggle up to
shifting continents and
ocean currents. Swap tonnage
and compare monsoons.

Even Chemistry. Someone
tangible. Flasks, bubblings
and a low flame underneath.
With someone warm like this
I'd take my chances.

Maths would find in me no questions
English Lit. no answers.

A task completed everyday
keeps sin and boredom both at bay
is what his mother used to say.

In a shop doorway
at the back of Skelhorne Street
a man in his early forties
grinning and muttering
is buttering a piece of bacon
with a pair of rusty scissors.
They are only nail scissors
and he has difficulty holding them
in his clumsy, larded hands.

The next day will be spent
untying the little knots.

In Renshaw Street
a man with blue eyes
and skin the colour of worn pavements
burrows into the busstop litterbin.
The sherrybottle is empty
but there is a bacon rasher
and a screwedup foil of Lurpak
as well as a deflated ball of string.

String is great.
It ties up pillowends
and keeps the wind
out of your trouserlegs.
Things dont get lost
when there's string about.
Good to play with in bed.
Always keep some handy.

Near Windsor Street
where they are pulling down houses
there is much that rusts and glistens.
A pair of nail scissors
halfhidden by tin cans, stands,
one foot in the grave.
Approaching is a man
tying a rosary of knots into a length of dirty string.

His life, like this poem,
out of sequence,
a series of impressions,
unfinished, imperfect.

Three Rusty Nails

Mother, there's a strange man
Waiting at the door
With a familiar sort of face
You feel you've seen before.

Says his name is Jesus
Can we spare a couple of bob
Says he's been made redundant
And now can't find a job.

Yes I think he is a foreigner
Egyptian or a Jew
Oh aye, and that reminds me
He'd like some water too.

Well shall I give him what he wants
Or send him on his way?
O.K. I'll give him 5p
Say that's all we've got today.

And I'll forget about the water
I suppose it's a bit unfair
But honest, he's filthy dirty
All beard and straggly hair.

* * *

Mother, he asked about the water
I said the tank had burst
Anyway I gave him the coppers
That seemed to quench his thirst.

He said it was little things like that
That kept him on the rails
Then he gave me his autographed picture
And these three rusty nails.

cosy biscuit

What I wouldn't give for a nine to five.
Biscuits in the right hand drawer,
teabreaks, and typists to mentally undress.

The same faces. Somewhere to hang
your hat and shake your umbrella.
Cosy.   Everything in its place.

Upgraded every few years. Hobbies.
Glass of beer at lunchtime
Pension to look forward to.

Two kids.   Homeloving wife.
Bit on the side when the occasion arises
H.P.   Nothing fancy.   Neat semi.

* * *

What I wouldn't give for a nine to five.
Glass of beer in the right hand drawer
H.P. on everything at lunchtime.

The same 2 kids. Somewhere to hang
your wife and shake your bit on the side.
Teabreaks and a pension to mentally undress.

The same semifaces upgraded.
Hobbies every few years, neat typists
in wet macs when the umbrella arises.

What I wouldn't give for a cosy biscuit.

A Brown Paper Carrierbag

IN THE TIME . . .

    a spider's web woven across
    the plateglass window shivers snaps
    and sends a shimmering haze of lethal stars
    across the crowded restaurant

IN THE TIME IT TAKES . . .

    jigsaw pieces of shrapnel
    glide gently towards children
    tucking in   to   the warm flesh
    a terrible hunger sated

IN THE TIME IT TAKES TO PUT DOWN . . .

    on the pavement
    people come apart   slowly
    at first
    only the dead not screaming

IN THE TIME IT TAKES TO PUT DOWN
A BROWN PAPER CARRIERBAG.

He who owns the Whistle, rules the World

january wind and the sun
playing truant again.
Rain beginning to scratch
its fingernails across
the blackboard sky

in the playground
kids divebomb, corner
at Silverstone or execute
traitors. Armed
with my Acme Thunderer
I step outside,
take a deep breath
and bring the world
to a standstill

Catching up on Sleep

i go to bed early
to catch up on my sleep
　　　but my sleep
is a slippery customer
it bobs and weaves
　　　and leaves
me exhausted. It
side steps my clumsy tackles
with ease.　　Bed
raggled I drag
myself to my knees.

The sheep are countless
I pretend to snore
yearn for chloroform
or a sock on the jaw
body sweats heart beats
there is Panic in the Sheets
until
as dawn slopes up the stairs
to set me free
unawares
sleep catches up on me

Nocturne

Unable to sleep.
Every sound an enemy.
each stirring an intruder.

Even my own breathing
is frisked
before being allowed out.

I suffer during darkness
a thousand bludgeonings,
see blood everywhere.

How my poor heart
dreads the night
shift. I wear

a smear of sweat
like a moist plastercast.
Adrift in a monstered sea.

Those actors who scare so well
in your nightmares
have all practised first on me.

The Lake

For years there have been no fish in the lake.
People hurrying through the park avoid it like the plague
Birds steer clear and the sedge of course has withered.
Trees lean away from it, and at night it reflects,
not the moon, but the blackness of its own depths.
There are no fish in the lake. But there is life there.
There is life . . .

Underwater pigs glide between reefs of coral debris.
They love it here. They breed and multiply
in sties hollowed out of the mud
and lined with mattresses and bedsprings.
They live on dead fish and rotting things,
drowned pets, plastic and assorted excreta.
Rusty cans they like the best.
Holding them in webbed trotters
their teeth tear easily through the tin
and poking in a snout
they noisily suck out
the putrid matter within.

There are no fish in the lake. But there is life there.
There is life . . .

For on certain evenings after dark
shoals of pigs surface and look out
at those houses near the park.
Where, in bathrooms, children feed stale bread
to plastic ducks, and in attics
toyyachts have long since runaground.
Where, in livingrooms, anglers dangle their lines
on patterned carpets, and bemoan the fate
of the ones that got away.

Down on the lake, piggy eyes glisten.
They have acquired a taste for flesh.
They are licking their lips. Listen . . .

The death of John Berryman in slow motion

We open on a frozen river
(the spot where the poet has arranged to meet death).
The whiteness is blinding.
The glare hurts our eyes.

From somewhere above he jumps.
We see the shadow first
seeping into the ice
like a bruise. Thickening.

There is no sound but the wind
skulking beneath the bridge.

Now the body comes into shot.
Falling, blurred, a ragged bearskin.
The shadow opens its arms to greet it.

The wind is holding its breath.

We freeze frame at the moment of impact
(noting the look of surprise on the poet's face).
We then pan slowly upwards
to the grey Minnesota sky.

Fade to black.

Take a poem, Miss Smith.

Take a poem, Miss Smith.
I will call it *The Ploughman*.
'The ploughman wearily follows the plough,
The dust that lies upon his brow,
Gnarled as the dead oak tree bough,
Makes me think of how . . . of how . . . '
How nice you smell, Miss Smith.
Is it Chanel? I thought so.
But to work: 'The ploughman wearily follows . . . '
Ah, but I am wearied of ploughing.
File it away under 'Nature — unfinished'.

Take a poem, Miss Smith.
It is entitled *Belfast*
'Along the Shankhill Road, a pall
Of smoke hangs, thick as . . . thick as . . . '
Hair, something different about the hair.
A new style? It suits you.
But where was I? Oh yes:
'Along the Shankhill Road . . . '
No, I feel unpolitical today.
Put it away in the file
marked 'Wars — unfinished'.

Take a poem, Miss Smith.
It will be known as *Flesh*.
'The flesh I love to touch
Is soft as . . . soft as . . . '
Take off your blouse, Miss Smith,
I feel a love poem coming on . . .

His poems are nets

His poems are nets
in which he hopes
to capture girls

He makes them at work
or late at night
when pubs are closed

He uses materials
at hand. Scraps
of conversation, jokes,

lines lifted from
dead poets (he likes
a bit of poetry in his poems)

* * *

He washes his hair
for the reading
and wears tight pants

When it comes to him
he swaggers out
unzipping his file

Exposes small dreams
which he breaks
with a big stick

His verse a mag
nifying glass
held up to his prick

* * *

His poems are nets
and like nets
can be seen through

Girls bide their time
Wait for the singer
to throw them a line.

Blazing Fruit
(or The Role of the Poet as Entertainer)

During dinner the table caught fire.
No one alluded to the fact
and we ate on, regardless of
the flames singeing our conversation.

Unaware of the smoke
and the butlers swooning,
topics ranged from Auden
to Zefferelli. I was losing
concentration however, and being
short on etiquette, became tense
and began to fidget with the melting cutlery.

I was fashioning a spoon
into a question mark
when the Chablis began to steam
and bubble. I stood up,
mumbled something about having left the gas running
and fled blushing
across the plush terrain of the carpet.

The tut-tut-tutting could be heard above
the cra-cra-cracking of the bone china.

Outside, I caught a cab
to the nearest bus stop.
While, back at the table,
they were toying with blazing fruit
and discussing the Role of the Poet as Entertainer,
when the roof fell in.

Poem for a dead poet

He was a poet he was.
A proper poet.
He said things
that made you think
and said them nicely.
He saw things
that you or I
could never see
and saw them clearly.
He had a way
with language.
Images flocked around
him like birds,
St Francis, he was,
of the words. Words?
Why he could almost make 'em talk.

Mouth

I went to the mirror
but the mirror was bare,
looked for my mouth
but my mouth wasn't there.
Over the lips had grown
a whiskered hymen of skin.

I went to the window
wanting to shout
I pictured the words
but nothing came out.
The face beneath the nose
an empty hoarding.

And as I waited, I could feel
flesh filling in the space behind.
Teeth melted away tasting of snow
as the stalactites of the palate
joined the stalagmites below.
The tongue, like a salted snail,
sweated and shrivelled.

The doctor has suggested plastic surgery:
a neat incision, cosmetic dentistry
and full red lips.
He meant well but I declined.

After all, there are advantages.
At last I have given up smoking,
and though food is a needle
twice a day, it needs no cooking.
There is little that I miss.
I never could whistle and there's no one to kiss.

In the street, people pass by
unconcerned. I give no one directions
and in return am given none.
When asked if I am happy
I look the inquisitor straight in the eye
and think to myself . . . ("

Cabbage
(after 'I like that stuff' by Adrian Mitchell)

Humphrey Bogart died of it
People are terrified of it
cancer
I hate that stuff

Peter Sellers was laid low with it
one in five of us will go with it
heart attack
I hate that stuff

Monroe's life turned sour on it
Hancock spent his last half hour on it
sleeping pills
I hate that stuff

Jimi Hendrix couldn't wait for it
Chemistshops stay open late for it
heroin
I hate that stuff

Mama Cass choked on it
Blankets get soaked in it
vomit
I hate that stuff

Women learn to live with it
No one can live without it
blood
I hate that stuff

Hospitals are packed with it
Saw my mother racked with it
                    pain
          I hate that stuff

Few like to face the truth of it
We're all living proof of it
                    death
          I hate that stuff

Schoolkids are forcefed with it
Cattle are served dead with it
                    cabbage
          I hate that stuff

War of the Roses

Friday came the news.
Her G.P. rang and told her.
The telephone buckled
in her hand. Safely distanced,
he offered to come round.
'Why bother,' she said, 'Bastard.'

She had guessed anyway. The body
had been telling her for months.
Sending haemorrhages, eerie messages
of bruises. Outward signs
of inner turmoil. You can't sweep
blood under the carpet.

Thirty, single, living with and for
a four-year-old daughter. Smokes,
drinks whisky, works in television.
Wakes around four each morning
fearful and crying. Listens to
the rioting in her veins.

Her blood is at war with itself.
With each campaign more pain,
a War of the Roses over again.
She is a battlefield. In her,
Red and White armies compete.
She is a pair of crossed swords
on the medical map of her street.

Survivor

Everyday
I think about dying.
About disease, starvation,
violence, terrorism, war,
the end of the world.

It helps
keep my mind off things.

Just another Autumn day

In Parliament, the Minister
for Mists and Mellow Fruitfulness
announces, that owing to
inflation and rising costs
there will be no Autumn
next year. September, October
and November are to be
cancelled, and the Government
to bring in the nine-month year instead.
Thus will we all live longer.

Emergency measures are to be
introduced to combat outbreaks
of well-being, and feelings
of elation inspired by the season.
Breathtaking sunsets will be
restricted to alternate Fridays
and gentle dusks prohibited.
Fallen leaves will be outlawed
and persons found in possession
of conkers, imprisoned without trial.
Thus will we all work harder.

The announcement caused little reaction.
People either way don't really care
No time have they to stand and stare
Looking for work or slaving away
Just another Autumn day.

Incident at a Presidential Garden Party

Taking tea in front of the White House.
Uninvited, a forty-ton diesel truck
Bursts through the railings
and skids across the lawn.

Tables are turned. Salads tossed
to the grass, canapes to the wind.
Colonels and creamcakes
squelch in the mad career.

Senators scream, tyres squeal,
underlings crunched underwheel.
Out of control, the juggernaut
surges towards the President.

No one moves. Slow motion now,
as in a dream. Half-smiling
he turns to face it. Smash.
Smithereens.   Then silence.

The Great Man dusts his suit
ensures his tie is straight.
The truck is given the kiss of life.
But too late.

May Ball

The evening lay before us
like her silken dress
arranged carefully over the bed.
It would be a night to remember.
We would speak of it often
in years to come. There would
be good food and wine,
cabaret, and music to dance to.
How we'd dance.
How we'd laugh.
We would kiss indiscreetly,
and what are lawns for
but to run barefoot across?

But the evening didn't do
what it was told.
It's the morning after now
and morningafter cold.
I don't know what went wrong
but I blame her. After all
I bought the tickets.
Of course, I make no mention,
that's not my style,
and I'll continue to write
at least for a while.
I carry her suitcase down to the hall,
our first (and her last) University Ball.

Closet Fascist

in the staffroom
or over drinks
he says the things
with which he thinks
his colleagues will concur:
anti-Fascist, anti-Front
liberalminded, fair.

But enthroned alone
in his W.C.
on toilet paper
signs a decree
deporting immigrants en masse.
Salutes the mob
then wipes his ass.

Solarium

i own a solarium
and when it's cold
i simmer in
artificial gold

i keep away
from mornings grey
my private sun
smiles down all day

i pity those
whose flesh is white
as bronzed i sleep
alone each night

Passion

We keep our noses clean, my friend and i,
do what we're told.
Keep profiles soft and low
as we grow old.

We take up little space, my friend and i,
avoid the town.
Keep our curtains drawn
our voices down.

We live an ordered life, my friend and i,
cause little fuss.
If only everyone
could be like us.

* * *

Screaming now, he screams, my friend, and i
know what to do.
Have him put away.
(Well wouldn't you?)

They bought the horse
in Portobello
brought it home
could hardly wait
installed it in the living room
next to knitted dinner plate

Next to ashtray
(formerly bedpan)
euphonium
no one can play
camel-saddle dollypeg
wooden gollywog with tray

Near a neo
deco lampshade
(a snip at
thirty-seven quid)
castanets and hula-hoop
trunk with psychedelic lid

Under front end
of a caribou
next to foam-
filled rollerskate
(made by a girl in Camden Lock
— she of knitted dinner plate)

Uprooted from
its carousel
the painted horse
now laid to waste
amidst expensive bric-à-brac
and sterile secondhand bad taste

* * *

And each night as Mr and Ms Trend
in brassbed they lie dreaming
the horse in downstairs darkness
mouths a silent screaming.

We live a simple life
my wife and I. Are
the envy of our friends.
We are artists. Skilled craftsmen.
I am good with my hands
She with hers.
I am a goldsmith
She a masseuse.

I design and make
gold lockets that cannot be opened
necklaces that will not fasten
ornate keys for which there are no locks.
Trinkets to buy and hoard
toys for the rich and bored.
Things useless, but beautiful.

Compared with the objects I make,
I am dull.
My wife is not dull,
She is exciting.
After a hard day at the parlor
or visiting hotels
(I do not pry)
She comes home
tired, but exciting.

I give her something golden
each evening something new.
It makes her smile.
She rewards me with her golden body
which I melt and shape at will.
Fashioning, with consummate skill,
the precious metal of her flesh.

We live a golden life
my wife and I. Dream
golden dreams. And
each golden morning
go our golden ways.
Make golden dreams for strangers.
Golden nights
and golden days.

The Rot

Some years ago the Rot set in.
It began in a corner of the bedroom
following the birth of the second child.
It spread into the linen cupboard
and across the fabric of our lives.
Experts came to treat it.
Could not.
The Rot could not be stopped.

Dying now, we live with it.
The fungus grows.
It spreads across our faces.
We watch the smiles rot,
gestures crumble.
Diseased, we become the disease.
Part of the fungus.
The part that dreams. That feels pain.

We are condemned.
Things dying, that flaunt their dying,
that cannot hide, are demolished.
We will rot eachother no longer.
From the street outside
comes the sound of the drill,
as men, hungry for dust,
close in for the kill.

10 Ways to Make a Killing

1 Get out of bed early and frequently.
   Remember, punctuality is the investor's best friend.

2 Resist the temptation to dress too gaudily.

3 Keep your figures neat and your columns orderly.

4 Avoid fatty foods.

5 Whatever you do . . . Whichever way we . . . I mean.

6 Your face. I think of your face. Your body.

7 Enfranchise non-voting 'A' shares through a rights
   issue.

8 Pain. The tears. But the laughter. We must never
   forget the laughter.

9 Not too late. Don't leave me. Please don't leave . . .

10

Holiday on Death Row

I

new dead flowers in

living room. First

Wasp of Spring. Time

for writing. Sap and

dying. Ashes and seed

lie scattered etc.

In kitchen, Wife

cook sunday dinner

for herself. Upstairs

Husband push drawing

pins into scowling

mouth of penis.

2

Wife is out. Has taken

clichés to launderette.

Husband, withdrawn, stare

overlong at photographs

of himself, in hope

of being recognised.

In front of mirrors

he bob and weave,

turn suddenly to catch

reflection off guard.

Reflection always on time.

On occasions, lying in wait.

3

Wife, downstairs midnight

putting cholesterol in his

Flora, decide their life

together has become anathema.

Stuffed toad in birdcage.

Husband, upstairs writing

poems she will never

read, decide holiday

abroad would be best

thing for both of them.

Next day he leave for Anathema.

Wife give toad kiss of life.

4

Husband, penis loaded

with drawing pins, swagger

into kitchen. Unimpressed,

Wife snarl matteroffactly.

'You rat a tat tat

    rat a tat tat

Take that a tat tat.'

Wife is pinned against wall

like fading Wanted Poster.

Husband pack away

empty shotgun and return

upstairs to collect reward.

5

she hang on his every word.

Pull, pull and pull.

Hands to his mouth

he fight back. Wife

drag him to floor.

Words cry out in pain:

'Words, we're only words,

we don't mean anything.'

Wife release grip

and return to kitchen.

'That what you always

say.' She say.

6

in Husband's dreams, her

stockings burst at seams.

She is centre-fold

of all his magazines.

Pinned up each night,

she disport herself

as he befit. As he

thought she used to do

or might have done.

Prickteasing series of

saucy pix. His memory

playing safe, playing tricks.

7

except for sound of their breathing.

In bed Husband mustn't touch.

Put arms around body he

helped shape. He fight impulse.

Do what is not natural.

Keep his self to himself.

Nerve ends tingle. He become

Electric Chair and move in.

She asleep on Death Row.

He wonder what would be

her last request. Chair

get erection. Chair know best.

8

Wife hoard hazelnuts

in cunt. Husband

train squirrels to

fetch hazelnuts. Wife

keep fox in petticoats

to chase squirrels. At

break of day, Husband,

in coat so gay, unleash

hounds in bedroom to catch

fox. Wife join Anti-blood-

sports League. Husband join

Anti-nuts-in-cunts Brigade.

9

Wife want life of own.

Husband want life of Wife.

Husband hire hitman.

Hitman hit Wife.

Wife hit back.

Hit, hitman run.

Wife run harder.

Hurt hitman.

Hurt hitman hit Husband.

Tired Husband hire second

hitman to fire first hitman.

Fired hitman retire, hurt.

10

Husband keep live rat down

front of jeans for rainy day.

One rainy day, drunk on

cooking sherry, Wife slip

hand inside Husband's jeans.

With brutal strokes she

skin it alive before

pulling off its head.

Wiping blood on pinny

she return to cakemix.

Husband bury dead rat

for another year.

I I

upstairs, Husband wrestle

with major themes. Wife

in kitchen putting

two and two together.

Always wife in kitchen

Always Husband wrestling.

On kitchen table is

flour, water, drawing pins,

salt, blood, ashes etc.

On desk upstairs,

major themes (or parts

thereof) lie scattered etc.

12

photographs of hitmen.

Hazelnuts for rainy day.

Dead flowers in fading

penis. Clichéd toad

bursting at seams. Empty

shotgun in birdcage. Holiday

on Death Row. Words,

we're only words.

Husband, upstairs, painting

out light in painting

of end of tunnel. Wife

in garden, digging up rat.

Rabbit in Mixer Survives

A baby rabbit fell into a quarry's mixing machine yesterday and came out in the middle of a concrete block. But the rabbit still had the strength to dig its way free before the block set.

The tiny creature was scooped up with 30 tons of sand, then swirled and pounded through the complete mixing process. Mr Michael Hooper, the machine operator, found the rabbit shivering on top of the solid concrete block, its coat stiff with fragments. A hole from the middle of the block and paw marks showed the escape route.

Mr Reginald Denslow, manager of J.R. Pratt and Sons' quarry at Kilmington, near Axminster, Devon, said: 'This rabbit must have a lot more than nine lives to go through this machine. I just don't know how it avoided being suffocated, ground, squashed or cut in half.' With the 30 tons of sand, it was dropped into a weighing hopper and carried by conveyor to an overhead mixer where it was whirled around with gallons of water.

From there the rabbit was swept to a machine which hammers wet concrete into blocks by pressure of 100 lb per square inch. The rabbit was encased in a block eighteen inches long, nine inches high and six inches thick. Finally the blocks were ejected on to the floor to dry and the dazed rabbit clawed itself free. 'We cleaned him up, dried him by the electric fire, then he hopped away,' Mr Denslow said.

Daily Telegraph

'Tell us a story Grandad'
The bunny rabbits implored
'About the block of concrete
Out of which you clawed.'

'Tell every gory detail
Of how you struggled free
From the teeth of the Iron Monster
And swam through a quicksand sea.'

'How you battled with the Humans
(And the part we like the most)
Your escape from the raging fire
When they held you there to roast.'

The old adventurer smiled
And waved a wrinkled paw
'All right children, settle down
I'll tell it just once more.'

His thin nose started twitching
Near-blind eyes began to flood
As the part that doesn't age
Drifted back to bunnyhood.

When spring was king of the seasons
And days were built to last
When thunder was merely thunder
Not a distant quarry blast.

How, leaving the warren one morning
Looking for somewhere to play
He'd wandered far into the woods
And there had lost his way.

When suddenly without warning
The earth gave way, and he fell
Off the very edge of the world
Into the darkness of Hell.

Sharp as the colour of a carrot
On a new-born bunny's tongue
Was the picture he recalled
Of that day when he was young.

Trance-formed now by the memory
His voice was close to tears
But the story he was telling
Was falling on deaf ears.

There was giggling and nudging
And lots of 'Sssh — he'll hear'
For it was a trick, a game they played
Grown crueller with each year.

'Poor old Grandad' they tittered
As they one by one withdrew
'He's told it all so often
He now believes it's true.'

Young rabbits need fresh carrots
And his had long grown stale
So they left the old campaigner
Imprisoned in his tale.

Petrified by memories
Haunting ever strong
Encased in a block of time
Eighteen inches long.

* * *

Alone in a field in Devon
An old rabbit is sitting, talking,
When out of the wood, at the edge of the world,
A man with a gun comes walking.

Six Shooters

You are his repartee.
His last word on the subject.

After each row
he storms upstairs
and takes you out of
the dressingtable drawer.

He points you
at the bedroom door
and waits for her
to dare one final taunt.

'Come on up' you croon.
'Come on up.'

2

She brazens it out.
Denies. Tries
to cover up
in a negligee of lies.

You, the lead hyphen
in between.
Infiltrator.

He loves her still
but she gone done him wrong.
You burst into song.

In a flash, all is forgiven.

3

Went through a war together
never left his side.

Back home, though illicit,
still his pride.

4 a.m. in the den now.
The note written. Suicide.

You don't care who
you kill do you?
With whom you fellate.

Into whose mouth
you hurl abuse,
whose brains you gurgitate.

4

After the outlaw
has bitten the dust
(Never again to rise)

The sheriff
takes you for a spin
round his finger

then blows the smoke
from your eyes.

5

You rarely get the blame.
Always the man
behind the hand
that holds you

Always the finger
in front of the trigger
you squeeze.

You rarely get the blame.
Always the fool
who thinks that you're
the answer

Always the tool
who does just as
you please.

6

oiled
and snug
in a
moist
holster

six
deadly pearls
in a
gross
oyster

Happy Ending

Out of the wood
at the edge of the world
a man with a gun
comes walking.
Feels not the sun
upon his face
nor hears a rabbit talking.

Over the edge
at the end of it all
the man stands
still as stone.
In his hands
the gun held
to his mouth like a microphone.

The rabbit
runs to safety
at the sudden cry
of pain.
As the man lets fly
a ferret
into the warren of his brain.

There Was a Knock on the Door. It Was the Meat.

There was a knock on the door.
It was the meat. I let it in.
Something freshly slaughtered
Dragged itself into the hall.

Into the living-room it crawled.
I followed. Though headless,
It headed for the kitchen
As if following a scent.

Straight to the oven it went
And lay there. Oozing softly to itself.
Though moved, I moved inside
And opened wide the door.

I switched to Gas Mark Four.
Set the timer. And grasping
The visitor by a stump
Humped it home and dry.

Did I detect a gentle sigh?
A thank you? The thought that I
Had helped a thing in need
Cheered me as I turned up the heat.

Two hours later the bell rang.
It was the meat.

The Birderman

Most weekends, starting in the spring
Until late summer, I spend angling.
Not for fish. I find that far too tame
But for birds, a much more interesting game.

A juicy worm I use as bait
Cast a line into the tree and wait.
Seldom for long (that's half the fun)
A commotion in the leaves, the job's half done.

Pull hard, jerk home the hook
Then reel him in. Let's have a look . . .
A tiny thing, a fledgling, young enough to spare.
I show mercy. Unhook, and toss it to the air.

It flies nestwards and disappears among the leaves
(What man roasts and braises, he too reprieves).
What next? A magpie. Note the splendid tail.
I wring its neck. Though stringy, it'll pass for quail.

Unlike water, the depths of trees are high
So, standing back, I cast into the sky.
And ledger there beyond the topmost bough,
Until threshing down, like a black cape, screams a crow!

Evil creature! A witch in feathered form.
I try to net the dark, encircling storm.
It caws for help. Its cronies gather round
They curse and swoop. I hold my ground.

An infernal mass, a black, horrific army
I'll not succumb to Satan's origami.
I reach into my coat, I've come prepared,
Bring out my pocket scarecrow — Watch out bird!

It's cross-shaped, the sign the godless fear
In a thunderflap of wings they disappear.
Except of course, that one, ungainly kite
Broken now, and quickly losing height.

I haul it in, and with a single blow
Dispatch it to that Aviary below.
The ebb and flow: magpie, thrush, nightingale and crow.
The wood darkens. Time to go.

I pack away the food I've caught
And thankful for a good day's sport
Amble home. The forest fisherman.
And I'll return as soon as I can

To bird. For I'm a birderer. The birderman.

When I Am Dead

I could never begin a poem: 'When I am dead'
As several poets still alive have done.
The jokey Last Will, and litanies
Of things we are to do when they are gone.

Courageous stuff. Written I shouldn't wonder
The Morning After, in the throes
Of grim despair. Head still ringing from the noise
Of nights keeling over like glass dominoes.

The chill fear that perhaps the writer
Might outlive the verse, provides the spur
To nail the spectre down in print,
To risk a sort of atheistic prayer.

God, of course, does not appear in rhyme,
Poets of our time being more inclined
To dwell upon the price of manuscripts
And how they want the coffin lined.

Or ashes scattered, cats fed, ex-wives
Gunned down. Meanwhile, in a drawer
Neat and tidy, the bona fide Will,
Drawn-up and witnessed by an old family lawyer.

And though poets I admire have published poems
Whose imperfections reflect our own decay,
I could never begin a poem: 'When I am dead'
In case it tempted Fate, and Fate gave way.

A Visit to the Poet and his Wife

To set the scene: A cave
in Madron, Cornwall.
On a warm September afternoon
Mr and Mrs W. S. G. are 'at home'
to admirers bearing distilled gifts.

Mine host, after clearing
a mess of mss from the table
takes *implements in their places*
from its place, and puts on
spectacles to clear the air.

A warm, brown voice
with silver whiskers unveils
a poem that is the spilling
image of itself. The onlisteners
are amazed at its likeness.

Tumblers, half-filled with malt,
are topped up with bright
watery sunshine by the good
Lady of the Cottage. The afternoon
saddens at its own passing.

To set the scene: A cave
in Madron, Cornwall.
On a warm September afternoon
Mr and Mrs W.S.G. are 'at home'
to admirers bearing distilled gifts.

The Examination
(written at the Arvon Foundation,
Totleigh Barton, Devon)

'Well doctor, what do you think?'
He took the poem and examined it.
'Mmmm . . .'
The clock ticked nervously.
'This will have to come out for a start.'
He stabbed a cold finger into its heart.
'Needs cutting here as well.
This can go.
And this is weak. Needs building up.'
He paused . . .
'But it's the Caesura I'm afraid,
Can't do much about that.'
My palms sweated.
'Throw it away and start again, that's my advice.
And on the way out, send in the next patient, will you?'

I buttoned up my manuscript and left.
Outside, it was raining odes and stanzas.
I caught a crowded anthology and went directly home.

Realizing finally that I would never be published.
That I was to remain one of the alltime great
    unknown poets,
My work rejected by even the vanity presses,
I decided to end it all.

Taking an overdose of Lyricism
I awaited the final peace
When into the room burst the Verse Squad
Followed by the Poetry Police.

Framed

In the Art Gallery
it is after closing time
everybody has left
except a girl
who is undressing
in front of a large painting
entitled: 'Nude'

(The girl undressing
is the girl in the painting)

naked now she faces
the girl who gazes
out at the girl
who naked faces
the girl who
naked gazes out

of the picture
steps the nude
who smiles, dresses and walks away
leaving the naked girl
gazing into the empty space
Framed   by this poem.

Noah's Arc

In my fallout shelter I have enough food
For at least three months. Some books,
Scrabble, and games for the children.
Calor gas and candles. Comfortable beds
And a chemical toilet. Under lock and key
The tools necessary for a life after death.
I have carried out my instructions to the letter.

Most evenings I'm down here. Checking the stores,
Our suits, breathing apparatus. Cleaning
And polishing. My wife, bless her,
Thinks I'm obsessive — like other men
About cars or football. But deep down
She understands. I have no hobbies.
My sole interest is survival.

Every few weeks we have what I call D.D.,
Or Disaster Drill. At the sound of the alarm
We each go about our separate duties:
Disconnecting services, switching off the mains,
Filling the casks with fresh water, etc.
Mine is to oversee everything before finally
Shooting the dog. (This I mime in private.)

At first, the young ones enjoyed the days
And nights spent below. It was an adventure.
But now they're at a difficult age
And regard extinction as the boring concern
Of grown-ups. Like divorce and accountancy.
But I am firm. Daddy knows best
And one fine day they'll grow to thank me.

Beneath my bunk I keep an Armalite rifle
Loaded and ready to use one fine day
When panicking neighbours and so-called friends
Try to clamber aboard. The ones who scoff,
Who ignore the signs. I have my orders,
There will be no stowaways. No gatecrashers
At my party. A party starting soon.

And the sooner the better. Like a grounded
Astronaut I grow daily more impatient.
Am on tenterhooks. Each night
I ask the Lord to get on with it.
I fear sometimes He has forsaken us,
We His favourite children. Meek, drilled,
And ready to inherit an earth, newly-cleansed.

I scan the headlines, watch the screen.
A doctor thrilling at each fresh tumour:
The latest invasion, a breakdown of talks.
I pray for malignancy. The self-induced
Sickness for which there is only one cure:
Radium treatment. The final absolution.
That part of full circle we have yet to come.

Waving at Trains

Do people who wave at trains
Wave at the driver, or at the train itself?
Or, do people who wave at trains
Wave at the passengers? Those hurtling strangers,
The unidentifiable flying faces?

They must think we like being waved at.
Children do perhaps, and alone
In a compartment, the occasional passenger
Who is himself a secret waver at trains.
But most of us are unimpressed.

Some even think they're daft.
Stuck out there in a field, grinning.
But our ignoring them, our blank faces,
Even our pulled tongues and up you signs
Come three miles further down the line.

Out of harm's way by then
They continue their walk.
Refreshed and made pure, by the mistaken belief
That their love has been returned,
Because they have not seen it rejected.

It's like God in a way. Another day
Another universe. Always off somewhere.
And left behind, the faithful few,
Stuck out there. Not a care in the world.
All innocence. Arms in the air. Waving.

Kisses and Blows

This is the water
cold and black
that drowned the child
that climbed on its back

This is the tree
badtempered and tall
that tripped the child
and made it fall

This is the cave
with rotting breath
that hid the child
and starved it to death

This is the mother
who one day chose
to smother the child
with kisses, and blows and blows and blows.

What My Lady Did

I asked my lady what she did
  She gave me a silver flute and smiled.
A musician I guessed, yes that would explain
  Her temperament so wild.

I asked my lady what she did
  She gave me a comb inlaid with pearl.
A hairdresser I guessed, yes that would explain
  Each soft and billowing curl.

I asked my lady what she did
  She gave me a skein of wool and left.
A weaver I guessed, yes that would explain
  Her fingers long and deft.

I asked my lady what she did
  She gave me a slipper trimmed with lace.
A dancer I guessed, yes that would explain
  Her suppleness and grace.

I asked my lady what she did
  She gave me a picture not yet dry.
A painter I guessed, yes that would explain
  The steadiness of her eye.

I asked my lady what she did
  She gave me a fountain pen of gold.
A poet I guessed, yes that would explain
  The strange stories that she told.

I asked my lady what she did
  She told me — and oh, the grief!
I should have guessed, she's under arrest
  My lady was a thief!

Romantic

I'm a romantic.
I often want to bring you flowers
Leave notes under the pillow.
Billets doux. Fivers.

I'm a romantic.
Many's the time I've nearly bought
the unexpected gift.
Chocolates. Diamonds.

I'm a romantic.
How often do I think
of surprising you at the sink.
Pulling the wool over your eyes.

I'm a romantic.
Love on the lino: soapy chocolates,
Diamonds, crushed flowers, fivers,
Billets doux. Wool.

(Little packet, two-thirds full.)

You and I

I explain quietly. You
hear me shouting. You
try a new tack. I
feel old wounds reopen.

You see both sides. I
see your blinkers. I
am placatory. You
sense a new selfishness.

I am a dove. You
recognize the hawk. You
offer an olive branch. I
feel the thorns.

You bleed. I
see crocodile tears. I
withdraw. You
reel from the impact.

Unlucky For Some

I

What do I do for a living? Survive.

Simple as that. 'God helps those

who help themselves.' That's what the

vicar told me. So I went into

the supermarket and helped myself.

Got six months. God help those

who help themselves. Nowadays

I'm a traveller. South-west mainly

then back here for the winter.

I like the open air. Plenty of it

and it's free. Everything else I beg

borrow or steal. Keep just about alive.

What do I do for a living? Survive.

2

It runs like duck's water off me back.

What people say. How do they know?

They seem to think I enjoy

looking shabby. Having no money.

Being moved on from cafés,

from warm places. How would

they like it? They'd soon sneer

on the other side of their faces

if they ended up down and out.

Up down and out. Up and down.

Out of luck. That's all you have to be.

Half of them calling the kettle black.

It runs like duck's water off me back.

3

It's the addicts I can't stand.

Getting drunk on pills. Stoned

they call it. Make me sick.

Sticking needles into themselves

in dirty lavatories. Got no shame.

And they get prescriptions. Wish

my doctor would give me one

everytime I felt like a drink.

I could take it along to the

allnight off-licence in Piccadilly

come back here and get drunk

for a week. Get high. Stoned.

It's the addicts I can't stand.

4

I'm no good, that's what I've been told

ever since I can remember. So

I try to live up to my reputation.

Or down to it. Thievin mainly.

And drugs. You get used to prison.

Don't like it though, being cooped up.

That's why I couldn't work in a shop

or a factory. Drive me crazy.

Can't settle down. 21 years old

and I look 40. It's the drugs.

I'll O.D. probably. Couldn't care less.

Rather die young than grow old.

I'm no good, that's what I've been told.

5

Now I'm one of the idle poor.

A rose in a garden of weeds.

Slightly shrivelled of course, but nevertheless

an interesting species: *'Retrobata inebriata'*.

I was born into the leisured classes.

No doubt you can tell. Born rich

and married rich as well. Too much

leisure that was the trouble. And drink.

Cost me a husband, home, family.

Now I've only a bed, a roof over my head.

Perhaps I don't deserve more.

I used to be one of the idle rich.

Now I'm one of the idle poor.

6

I get frightened you see. Easily scared.

Trouble is, I know what's goin on.

The things they've got planned.

The others don't understand, you see.

They say: 'What are you scared of?

There's no need to be frightened.'

I huddle myself up against

the window sometimes. Like a curtain.

Listening to what's goin on outside.

I've got X-ray hearin, you see.

It stretches for miles. When people

talk about me, I can hear every word.

I get frightened you see. Easily scared.

7

First and foremost I need a coat.

The one I'm wearing's got patches

on the patches. I can't go

for interviews dressed like this.

What sort of a job do you think

I'd get? A job as a tramp?

No thank you. And while I'm here

I need some vests and knickers.

None of them fancy ones either.

And shoes. Two pair. Leather.

Don't argue, I know my rights.

Refuse and I'll take you to court.

First and foremost I need a coat.

8

I try to take up little space.

Keep myself to myself. I find

the best way to get by is to say

nothing. Don't argue, don't interfere.

When there's trouble lie low.

That's why I wear a lot of grey.

Helps me hide away. Blend in

against the background. I eat

very little. Don't smoke or drink.

Get through the day unnoticed

that's the trick. The way to heaven.

Say me prayers each night just in case.

I try to take up little space.

9

It may sound silly but it's true.

I drink like there was no tomorrow

and I can't stand the taste of the stuff.

Never have. My mother was a drunk

and the smell of her was enough.

I drink to forget. I know it's a cliché

but it's true. I drink to forget

and I do. Occasionally I remember

what I was trying not to remember

but by then I've remembered

to drink, in order to make

myself forget. And I do.

It may sound silly but it's true.

10

I would have liked children I suppose.

A family and that. It's natural.

But it's too late now. Too old.

And trouble is I never liked men.

If I'd been born pretty

or with a nice figure, I might

have liked them then. Men,

and sex and that. But I'm

no oil painting. Had to face

that fact right from the start.

And you see, if you're born ugly

well that's the way life goes. But

I would have liked children I suppose.

11

Oh no, I don't have to be here.

I'm not a cast-off like the rest.

I'm one of the lucky ones. I've got

children. Both grown up. A son

and daughter who'd be only too pleased

to have me living with them.

But I prefer my independence.

Besides, they've got their own lives.

I'd only have to pick up the phone

and they'd be over. Or send money.

I mean, I could afford a room

in a nice clean hotel somewhere.

Oh no, I don't have to be here.

12

Things are better now with me new glasses.

I got the last pair just after the war

and I think they'd lost their power.

If I could read I'd be able

to read even better now. Everything's

so much clearer. Faces and places.

Television's improved too. Not

that I'm one for stayin in.

I prefer to be out and about.

Sightseein and windowshoppin.

In and out of the traffic.

If you keep on the move, time soon passes.

Things are better now, with me new glasses.

13

I always wanted to go on the stage.

Dancer mainly, though I had a lovely voice.

Ran away to the bright lights of London

to be a star. Nothing came of it though,

so I went on the game. An actress

of sorts you might say. I'm the oldest

professional in the oldest profession.

Would you like to see me dance?

I'll dance for you. I dance in here

all the time. The girls love it.

Do you like my dancing? Round

and round. Not bad eh? For my age.

I always wanted to go on the stage.

Beware January,
His greeting is a grey chill.
Dark stranger. First in at the kill.
    Get out while you can.

Beware February,
Jolly snowman. But beneath the snow
A grinning skeleton, a scarecrow.
    Don't be drawn into that web.

Beware March,
Mad Piper in a many-coloured coat
Who will play a jig then rip your throat.
    If you leave home, don't go far.

Beware April,
Who sucks eggs and tramples nests.
From the wind that molests
    There is no escape.

Beware May,
Darling scalpel, gall and wormwood.
Scented blossom hides the smell
    Of blood. Keep away.

Beware June,
Black lipstick, bruise-coloured rouge,
Sirensong and subterfuge.
    The wide-eyed crazed hypnotic moon.

Beware July,
Its juices overflow. Lover of excess
Overripe in flyblown dress.
    Insatiable and cruel.

Beware August,
The finger that will scorch and blind
Also beckons. The only place you'll find
    To cool off is the morgue.

Beware September,
Who speaks softly with honeyed breath.
You promise fruitfulness. But death
    Is the only gift that she'll accept.

Beware October,
Whose scythe is keenest. The old crone
Makes the earth tremble and moan.
    She's mean and won't be mocked.

Beware November,
Whose teeth are sharpened on cemetery stones,
Who will trip you up and crunch your bones.
    Iron fist in iron glove.

Beware December,
False beard that hides a sneer.
Child-hater. In what year
    Will we know peace?

The Jogger's Song

After leaving the Harp nightclub in Deptford, a 35-year-old woman was raped and assaulted by two men in Fordham Park. Left in a shocked and dishevelled state she appealed for help to a man in a light-coloured track-suit who was out jogging. Instead of rescuing her, he also raped her.

Evening Standard

Well, she was asking for it.
Lyin there, cryin out,
dyin for it. Pissed of course.
Of course, nice girls don't.
Don't know who she was,
where from, didn't care.
Nor did she. Slut. Slut.

Now I look after myself. Fit.
Keep myself fit. Got
a good body. Good body. Slim.
Go to the gym. Keep in trim.
Girls like a man wiv a good body.
Strong arms, tight arse. Right
tart she was. Slut. Pissed.

Now I don't drink. No fear.
Like to keep a clear
head. Keep ahead. Like
I said, like to know what I'm doin
who I'm screwin (excuse language).
Not like her. Baggage. Half-
dressed, couldn't-care-less. Pissed.

Crawlin round beggin for it.
Lyin there, dyin for it.
Cryin. Cryin. Nice girls don't.
Right one she was. A raver.
At night, after dark,
on her own, in the park?
Well, do me a favour.

And tell me this:
If she didn't enjoy it,
why didn't she scream?

The End of Summer

It is the end of summer
The end of day and cool,
As children, holiday-sated,
Idle happily home from school.
Dusk is slow to gather
The pavements still are bright,
It is the end of summer
And a bag of dynamite

Is pushed behind the counter
Of a department store, and soon
A trembling hand will put an end
To an English afternoon.
The sun on rooftops gleaming
Underlines the need to kill,
It is the end of summer
And all is cool, and still.

A Fair Day's Fiddle

Why can't the poor have the decency
to go around in bare feet?
Where's the pride that allows them
to fall behind on video recorders?

Such ostentation's indiscreet
when we can hardly afford as
much. They all smoke, of course,
and fiddle while the nation burns.

(Electric meters usually, and gas.)
And note, most have central heating.
Moonlighting's too romantic a word
for what's tantamount to cheating.

It's a question of priorities, I suppose,
give them money and it goes on booze.
Why can't the poor be seen to be poor?
Then we could praise the Lord, and give them shoes.

The Filmmaker
(with subtitles)

He was a filmmaker with a capital F.
Iconoclastic. He said 'Non' to Hollywood,   1
'Pourquoi? Ici je suis Le Chef.'   2
A director's director. Difficult but good.

But when Mademoiselle La Grande C.   3
Crept into his bed in Montparnasse
And kissed him on the rectum, he
Had a rectumectomy. But in vain. Hélas.   4

And how they mourned, the aficionados.
(Even stars he'd not met were seen to grieve,
The Christies, Fondas, Streeps and Bardots.)
And for them all, he'd one last trick up his sleeve.

'Cimetière Vérité' he called it (a final pun).   5
In a fashionable graveyard in Paris 3ième.
He was buried, and at the going down of the sun
Premiered his masterpiece, *La Mort, C'est Moi-même*.   6

The coffin, an oblong, lead-lined studio with space
For the body, a camera and enough light
To film in close-up that once sanguine face
Which fills the monumental screen each night.

The show is 'Un grand succès'. People never tire   7
Of filing past. And in reverential tone
They discuss the symbolism, and admire
Its honesty. *La Vérité* pared down to the bone.   8

FIN   9

1 'No.' 2 'Why? Here I am the chef.' 3 Miss the Big C. 4 Alas. 5 'True
cemetery' 6 *The Death it is Myself.* 7 'A grand success'. 8 The Truth   9 End

Happy Birthday

One morning as you step out of the bath
The telephone rings.
Wrapped loosely in a towel you answer it.

As you pick up the receiver
The front doorbell rings.
You ask the caller to hang on.

Going quickly into the hall
You open the door the merest fraction.
On the doorstep is a pleasing stranger.

'Would you mind waiting?' You explain,
'I'm on the telephone.' Closing the door to,
You hurry back to take the call.

The person at the other end is singing:
'Happy Birthday to you, Happy Birthday . . .'
You hear the front door click shut.

Footsteps in the hall.
You turn . . .

Last Lullaby

The wind is howling,
   My handsome, my darling,
An illwisher loiters
   Outside in the street.
The pain in your breastbone
   Tightens and tightens
And you are alone,
   My treasure, my sweet.

Gone is your lover,
   My angel, my dearest,
Gone to another
   To hold and caress.
Could that shadow you see
   On the curtain be me?
Of course not, beloved,
   Goodnight and God bless.

Are they not gentle,
   My naughty, my precious,
These hands that will bring you
   To sleep by and by?
Sweet dreams, my sweetheart,
   Hush, don't you cry.
Daddy will sing you
   A last lullaby.

Daddy will sing you
   A last lullaby.

All Over bar the Shouting

It's all over.
Almost a bar-room brawl.

Shouting does not become you.
Becomes you not at all.

It becomes me.
Shouting becomes me.

I become shouting.
I shout and shout and shout.

I shout until shouting
and I are one.

You walk out.
Leave me lock-

jawed in shout.
Dumbstuck.

Into the bar
the ghosts of years come streaming.

It's all over,
bar the shouting. Bar the screaming.

Q

I join the queue
We move up nicely.

I ask the lady in front
What are we queuing for.
'To join another queue,'
She explains.

'How pointless,' I say,
'I'm leaving.' She points
To another long queue.
'Then you must get in line.'

I join the queue.
We move up nicely.

Who Can Remember Emily Frying?

The Grand Old Duke of Wellington
Gave us the wellington boot.
The Earl of Sandwich, so they say,
Invented the sandwich. The suit

Blues saxophonists choose to wear
Is called after Zoot Sims (a Zoot suit).
And the inventor of the saxophone?
Mr Sax, of course. (Toot! Toot!)

And we all recall, no trouble at all,
That buccaneer, long since gone,
Famed for his one-legged underpants –
'Why, shiver me timbers' – Long John.

But who can remember Emily Frying?
(Forgotten, not being a man.)
For she it was who invented
The household frying pan.

And what about Hilary Teapot?
And her cousin, Charlotte Garden-Hose?
Who invented things to go inside birdcages
(You know, for budgies to swing on). Those.

The Host

He can sing and dance
Play piano, trumpet and guitar.
An amateur hypnotist
A passable ventriloquist
Can even walk a tightrope
(But not far). When contracted,
Can lend a hand to sleight-of
And juggling. Has never acted,
But is, none the less, a Star.

He has a young wife. His third.
(Ex-au pair and former
Swedish Beauty Queen)
And an ideal home
In the ideal home counties.
His friends are household
Names of stage and screen,
And his hobbies are golf,
And helping children of those
Less fortunate than himself
Get to the seaside.

Having been born again. And again.
He believes in God. And God
Certainly believes in him.
Each night before going to bed
He kneels in his den
And says a little prayer:
'Thank you Lord, for my work and play,
Please help me make it in the U.S.A.'

Then still kneeling, with head bowed,
He tries out new material
(Cleaned up, but only slightly).
And the Almighty laughs out loud
Especially at jokes about rabbis
And the Pope. Just one encore
Then time for beddy-byes.
So he stands, and he bows,
Blows a kiss to his Saviour,
Then dances upstairs to divide Scandinavia.

Sap

Spring again.
No denying the signs.
Rates bill. Crocuses on cue.
Daffodils rearing up
Like golden puff-adders.

Open to the neck, voices
Are louder. Unmuffled.
The lid lifted off the sky.
In the air, suddenly,
A feeling of *'je sais quoi'*.

I take the dog into the park.
Let myself off the lead.

Here I Am

Here I am
forty-seven years of age
and never having gone to work in ladies' underwear

Never run naked at night in the rain
Made love to a girl I'd just met on a plane

At that awkward age now between birth and death
I think of all the outrages unperpetrated
opportunities missed

The dragons unchased
The maidens unkissed
The wines still untasted
The oceans uncrossed
The fantasies wasted
The mad urges lost

Here I am
getting on for seventy
and never having stepped outside for a fight

Crossed on red, pissed on rosé (or white)
Pretty dull for a poet, I suppose, eh? Quite.

Today is Not a Day for Adultery

Today is not a day for adultery.
The sky is a wet blanket
Being shaken in anger. Thunder
Rumbles through the streets
Like malicious gossip.

Take my advice: braving
The storm will not impress your lover
When you turn up at the house
In an anorak. Wellingtons,
Even coloured, seldom arouse.

Your umbrella will leave a tell-tale
Puddle in the hall. Another stain
To be explained away. Stay in,
Keep your mucus to yourself.
Today is not a day for sin.

Best pick up the phone and cancel.
Postpone until the weather clears.
No point in getting soaked through.
At your age, a fuck's not worth
The chance of catching 'flu.

Bits of Me

When people ask: 'How are you?'
I say, 'Bits of me are fine.'
And they are. Lots of me I'd take
anywhere. Be proud to show off.

But it's the bits that can't be seen
that worry. The boys in the backroom
who never get introduced.
The ones with the Latin names

who grumble about the hours I keep
and bang on the ceiling
when I'm enjoying myself. The overseers.
The smug biders of time.

Over the years our lifestyles
have become incompatible.
We were never really suited
and now I think they want out.

One day, on cue, they'll down tools.
Then it's curtains for me. (Washable
plastic on three sides.) Post-op.
Pre-med. The bed nearest the door.

Enter cheerful staff nurse (Irish
preferably), 'And how are you today?'
(I see red.) Famous last words:
'Bits of me are fine.' On cue, dead.

Poem with a Limp

Woke up this morning with a
                                    limp.
Was it from playing
                        football
In my dreams? Arthrite's first
                                arrow?
Polio? Muscular dystrophy? (A bit of
                                        each?)

I staggered around the kitchen spilling
                                            coffee
Before hobbling to the bank for
                                    lire
For the holiday I knew I would not be
                                        taking.
(For Portofino read Stoke
                            Mandeville.)

Confined to a wheelchair for the
                                    remainder
Of my short and tragic life.
                                Wheeled
On stage to read my terse, honest
                                    poems
Without a trace of bitterness. 'How
                                    brave,

And smiling still, despite the
                              pain.'
Resigned now to a life of quiet
                              fortitude
I plan the nurses' audition.
                              Mid-afternoon
Sees me in the garden, sunning my
                              limp.

* * *

It feels a little easier now.
Perhaps a miracle is on its way?
(Lourdes, W11.)

By opening-time the cure is complete.
I rise from my deck-chair:
'Look, everybody, I can walk, I can walk.'

Melting into the Foreground

Head down and it's into the hangover.
Last night was a night best forgotten.
(Did you really kiss a man on the forehead?)

At first you were fine.
Melting into the foreground.
Unassuming. A good listener.

But listeners are speakers
Gagged by shyness
And soon the wine has
Pushed its velvet fingers down your throat.

You should have left then. Got your coat.
But no. You had the Taste.
Your newfound gift of garbled tongue
Seemed far too good to waste.

Like a vacuum-cleaner on heat
You careered hither and thither
Sucking up the smithereens
Of half-digested chat.

When not providing the lulls in conversation
Your strangled banter
Stumbled on to disbelieving ears.

Girls braved your leering incoherences
Being too polite to mock
(Although your charm was halitoxic,
Your wit, wet sand in a sock).

When not fawning over the hostess
You were falling over the furniture
(Helped to your feet, I recall,
By the man with the forehead).

Gauche attempts to prise telephone numbers
From happily married ladies
Did not go unnoticed.

Nor did pocketing a bottle of Bacardi
When trying to leave
In the best coat you could find.

I'd lie low if I were you.
Stay at home for a year or two.
Take up painting. Do something ceramic.
Failing that, emigrate to somewhere Islamic.

The best of luck whatever you do.
I'm baling out, you're on your own.
Cockpit blazing, out of control,
Into the hangover. Head down.

In Transit

She spends her life
in Departure Lounges,
flying from one to another.

Although planes frighten her,
baggage is a bother
and foreigners a bore,

in the stifled hysteria
of an airport
she, in transit, feels secure.

Enjoys the waiting game.
Cheered by storms, strikes
and news of long delays,

among strangers, nervous
and impatient for the off,
the old lady scrambles her days.

A Joy to be Old

It's a joy to be old.
Kids through school,
The dog dead and the car sold.

Worth their weight in gold,
Bus passes. Let asses rule.
It's a joy to be old.

The library when it's cold.
Immune from ridicule.
The dog dead and the car sold.

Time now to be bold.
Skinnydipping in the pool.
It's a joy to be old.

Death cannot be cajoled.
No rewinding the spool.
The dog dead and the car sold.

Get out and get arse'oled.
Have fun playing the fool.
It's a joy to be old.
The dog dead and the car sold.

Hundreds and Thousands

The sound of hounds
on red sand thundering

Hundreds and thousands
of mouths glistening

The blood quickening
Thunder and lightning

The hunted in dread
of the hundreds running

The sound of thunder
A white moon reddening

Thousands of mad hounds
on red sand marauding

Thundering onwards
in hundreds and thundreds

Thundreds and thundreds
Thundering   Thundering

Bars are Down

When I was a lad
most people round our way
were barzydown.

It was a world full of piecans.
Men who were barmy, married to women
who wanted their heads examined.

When not painting the railings,
our neighbours were doolally,
away for slates.

Or so my dad reckoned.
Needed locking away
the lot of them.

Leaving certain McGoughs
and a few close friends
free to walk the empty streets

in peace. Knowing exactly
whether we were coming or going.
Self-righteous in polished shoes.

Picking our way
clearheadedly,
between loose screws.

My Little Eye

The cord of my new dressing-gown
he helps me tie

Then on to my father's shoulder
held high

The world at night with my little eye
I spy

The moon close enough to touch
I try

Unheard of silver elephants have learned
to fly

Giants fence with searchlights
in the sky

Too soon into the magic shelter
he and I

Air raids are so much fun
I wonder why

In the bunk below, a big boy
starts to cry.

Bye Bye Black Sheep

Volunteering at seventeen, Uncle Joe
Went to Dunkirk as a Royal Marine
And lived, not to tell the tale.
Demobbed, he brought back a broken 303,
A quiver of bayonets, and a kitbag
Of badges, bullets and swastikas
Which he doled out among warstruck nephews.

With gasflame-blue eyes and dark unruly hair
He could have been God's gift. Gone anywhere.
But a lifetime's excitement had been used up
On his one-and-only trip abroad. Instead,
Did the pools and horses. 'Lash me, I'm bored,'
He'd moan, and use language when Gran
Was out of the room. He was our hero.

But not for long. Apparently he was
No good. Couldn't hold down a job.
Gave the old buck to his Elders and Betters.
Lazy as sin, he turned to drink
And ended up marrying a Protestant.
A regular black sheep was Uncle Joe.
Funny how wrong kids can be.

Insanity left him when he needed it most.
Forty years at Bryant & May, and a scroll
To prove it. Gold lettering, and a likeness
Of the Founder. Grandad's name writ small:
'William McGarry, faithful employee'.

A spent match by the time I knew him.
Choking on fish bones, talking to himself,
And walking round the block with a yardbrush
Over his shoulder. 'What for, Gran?' 'Hush . . .
Poor man, thinks he's marching off to war.

'Spitting image of Charlie, was your Grandad,
And taller too.' She'd sigh. 'Best-looking
Man in Seaforth. And straight-backed?
Why, he'd walk down Bridge Road
As if he had a coat-hanger in his suit.'

St Joseph's Hospice for the Dying
Is where Chaplin made his last movie.
He played Grandad, and gave a fine performance
Of a man raging against God, and cursing
The nuns and nurses who tried to hold him down.

Insanity left him when he needed it most.
The pillow taken from his face
At the moment of going under. Screaming
And fighting to regain the years denied,
His heart gave out, his mind gave in, he died.

The final scene brings tears to everybody's eyes.
In the parlour, among suppurating candles
And severed flowers, I see him smiling
Like I'd never seen him smile before.
Coat-hanger at his back. Marching off to war.

Hearts and Flowers

Aunty Marge,
Spinster of the parish, never had a boyfriend.
Never courted, never kissed.
A jerrybuilt dentist and a smashed jaw
Saw to that.

To her,
Life was a storm in a holy-water font
Across which she breezed
With all the grace and charm
Of a giraffe learning to windsurf.

But sweating
In the convent laundry, she would iron
Amices, albs and surplices
With such tenderness and care
You'd think priests were still inside.

Deep down,
She would like to have been a nun
And talked of missing her vocation
As if it were the last bus home:
'It passed me by when I was looking the other way.'

'Besides,'
She'd say, 'What Order would have me?
The Little Daughters of the Bingo?
The Holy Whist Sisters?' A glance at the ceiling.
'He's not that hard up.'

We'd laugh
And protest, knowing in our hearts that He wasn't.
But for the face she would have been out there,
Married, five kids, another on the way.
Celibacy a gift unearned, unasked for.

But though
A goose among grown-ups,
Let loose among kids
She was an exploding fireworks factory,
A runaway pantomime horse.

Everybody's
Favourite aunt. A cuddly toy adult
That sang loud and out of tune.
That dropped, knocked over and bumped into things,
That got ticked off just like us.

Next to
A game of cards she liked babysitting best.
Once the parents were out of the way
It was every child for itself. In charge,
Aunt Marge, renegade toddler-in-chief.

Falling
Asleep over pontoon, my sister and I,
Red-eyed, would beg to be taken to bed.
'Just one more game of snap,' she'd plead,
And magic two toffees from behind an ear.

Then suddenly
Whooshed upstairs in the time it takes
To open the front door. Leaving us to possum,
She'd tiptoe down with the fortnightly fib:
'Still fast asleep, not a murmur all night. Little angels.'

But angels
Unangelic, grew up and flew away. And fallen,
Looked for brighter toys. Each Christmas sent a card
With kisses, and wondered how she coped alone.
Up there in a council flat. No phone.

Her death
Was as quick as it was clumsy. Neighbours
Found the body, not us. Sitting there for days
Stiff in Sunday best. Coat half-buttoned, hat askew.
On her way to Mass. Late as usual.

Her rosary
Had snapped with the pain, the decades spilling,
Black beads trailing. The crucifix still
Clenched in her fist. Middle finger broken.
Branded into dead flesh, the sign of the cross.

From the missal
In her lap, holy pictures, like playing cards,
Lay scattered. Five were face-up:
A Full House of Sacred Hearts and Little Flowers.
Aunty Marge, lucky in cards.

TOWER HAMLETS COLLEGE LIBRARY
POPLAR CENTRE

Index of First Lines

a cat mistrusts the sun 75
A littlebit of heaven fell 24
A task completed everyday 114
after the battle of the Incriminating Loveletter 86
after the merrymaking, 78
After the outlaw 167
All night 106
As the cold winter evenings drew near 29
at first 80
at 7.55 this morning 103
at the goingdown of the sun 22
Aunty Marge, 228
away from you 52

Beware January, 198

Discretion is the better part of Valerie 72
Do people who wave at trains 180
Down first for breakfast 107
During dinner the table caught fire. 128

Everyday 135
except for sound of their breathing 154

First and foremost I need a coat. 191
For years there have been no fish in the lake. 122
Friday came the news. 134

Georgie Jennings was spit almighty. 96
Get out of bed early and frequently. 147
Girls are simply the prettiest things 74

harvesttime 91
He can sing and dance 210
He was a filmmaker with a capital F. 204
He was a poet he was. 129
Head down and it's into the hangover. 218
Here I am 213
Here is a poem for the two of us to play. 89
His poems are nets 126

233

Humphrey Bogart died of it 132
Husband keep live rat down 157
Husband, penis loaded 151

I always wanted to go on the stage. 197
I asked my lady what she did 182
I could never begin a poem: 'When I am dead' 174
I do not smile because I am happy. 93
I explain quietly.   You 184
I get frightened you see. Easily scared. 190
i go to bed early 120
i go to sleep on all fours 102
i have lately learned to swim 48
I join the queue 208
i once met a man 92
i own a solarium 140
i remember your hands 18
I try to take up little space. 192
i wanted one life 90
I went to the mirror 130
I would have liked children I suppose. 194
I'm a romantic. 183
I'm no good, that's what I've been told 188
in a corner of my bedroom 35
in bed 101
In Flanders fields in Northern France 20
in Husband's dreams, her 153
In my fallout shelter I have enough food 178
in october 60
In Parliament, the Minister 136
In the Art Gallery 177
in the no mans land 100
in the staffroom 139
IN THE TIME . . . 118
increasingly oftennow 37
Insanity left him when he needed it most. 226
it all started yesterday evening 58
it is afterwards 16
It is the end of summer 202
It may sound silly but it's true. 193
It runs like duck's water off me back. 186
It seems unlikely now 110
it wouldn't be wise to go away together 83

It's a joy to be old. 221

It's all over. 207

It's the addicts I can't stand. 187

january wind and the sun 119

last wednesday 82

lastnight 54

Let me die a youngman's death 15

'Look quickly!' said the stranger 66

Looks quite pretty lying there 17

lying in bed ofa weekdaymorning 98

middle   aged 84-5

midnight 104

monika the teathings are taking over! 57

monika who's been eating my porrage 56

Most weekends, starting in the spring 172

mother the wardrobe is full of infantrymen 23

Mother, there's a strange man 116

My busconductor tells me 31

Neat-haired and 79

new dead flowers in 148

Now I'm one of the idle poor. 189

Oh no, I don't have to be here. 195

oiled 169

ONCE I LIVED IN CAPITALS 112

One morning as you step out of the bath 205

Out of the wood 170

photographs of hitmen. 159

said i trusted you 55

saturdaymorning 47

She brazens it out. 165

she hang on his every word. 152

She is as beautiful as bustickets 70

She spends her life 220

snow crackles underfoot 67

So you think its Stephen? 94

Some years ago the Rot set in. 146

sometimes   34
sometimes at dawn you awake   50
Sometimes I dont smell so good.   109
spiders are holding their wintersports   108
Spring again.   212
Stoned and lonely in the union bar   113

Take a poem, Miss Smith.   125
Taking tea in front of the White House.   137
'Tell us a story Grandad'   161
ten milk bottles standing in the hall   46
The Act of Love lies somewhere   73
the baby   99
The cord of my new dressing-gown   224
The evening lay before us   138
The Grand Old Duke of Wellington   209
the littleman   32
The oldman in the cripplechair   30
The politicians,   28
The sound of hounds   222
The sun no longer loves me.   76
The wind is howling,   206
There was a knock on the door.   171
There's something sad   33
They bought the horse   142
they say the sun shone now and again   43
Things are better now with me new glasses.   196
This is the water   181
thismorning   77
To set the scene: A cave   175
Today is not a day for adultery.   214

Unable to sleep.   121
upstairs, Husband wrestle   158

Volunteering at seventeen, Uncle Joe   225

We keep our noses clean, my friend and i,   141
We live a simple life   144
We open on a frozen river   124
We sit in front of the wireless   87
'Well doctor, what do you think?'   176
Well, she was asking for it.   200

went through a war together 166
we've ignored eachother for a long time 64
What do I do for a living? Survive. 185
What I wouldn't give for a nine to five. 117
When i came to live with you 88
When I was a lad 223
When I was kneehigh to a tabletop, 62
When people ask: 'How are you?' 215
When the bus stopped suddenly 26
when you said you loved me 68
When you starred in *my* play 81
Why can't the poor have the decency 203
Wife, downstairs midnight 150
Wife hoard hazelnuts 155
Wife is out. Has taken 149
Wife want life of own. 156
Woke up this morning with a limp 216

yesterday 69
you always were a strange girl now weren't you? 36
You are his repartee. 164
you are so very beautiful 51
you are the cat's paw 38
You rarely get the blame. 168
you squeeze my hand and 49
your finger 53

TOWER HAMLETS COLLEGE LIBRARY

TOWER 11